French Letters

Letters

The Life and Loves of Miss Maxine Harrison

Eileen Fairweather

First published by Livewire Books, The Women's Press Ltd, 1987
A member of the Namara Group
34 Great Sutton Street, London EC1V 0DX

Reprinted 1987 (three times), 1988, 1993, 1998

Copyright © Eileen Faairweather 1987

British Library Cataloguing-in-Publication Data
French letters: the life and loves of Miss Maxine Harrison
    I. Title
    823'.914[F] PZ7

ISBN 0 7043 4951 5

Typeset in Bembo by MC Typeset Ltd, Kent
Printed and bound in Great Britain by Cox & Wyman Ltd,
Reading, Berkshire.

Miss Maxine Harrison
96 Sheraton Road
Hornsey
London N8
The South of England

August 20th

Miss Jean Oglethorpe
The Queen's Arms
Furnace Street
Ashton-under-Lyne
Lancashire
The Far North

Dear Jean,

This morning my eyes were so puffy from crying I looked like Kermit the Frog with a hangover. Since you deserted London to live in the middle of nowhere I've cried non stop. Mum says I'll soon find another best friend, but that just goes to show she's got no heart.

As for your parents, someone ought to report them to the Child Cruelty people. Fancy dragging you away from all your friends (i.e. me) just so they can run a rotten old pub in the rotten old North of England. What was wrong with the Hornsey Tavern? It's no excuse, your mum wanting to live closer to your ageing nan. Fifty-six isn't that ancient, Joan Collins is fifty-four and she's in *Dynasty*. It'll serve your parents right if you do run away.

Yes, I did ask my mum if she'd adopt you, but she says the law wouldn't allow it seeing as you're already fourteen and you belong to someone else. Trust her to take the easy way out.

Still – about our bet. Have you had time to size up the local talent yet, or have you been too busy since yesterday unpacking? I've got to admit I've been getting cold feet – about whether our bet's *moral* or not, I mean. I'll write more about that tomorrow. Right now I've got to get on with crying. I miss you terribly.

Yours faithfully,

Maxine Harrison (Miss)

Harrison's Betting Shop
c/o 96 Sheraton Road
London N8

August 21st

Dear Jean,

It's like this. I've been worrying all night about our bet and no offence but it *isn't* moral. When it comes to being the first to get a real boyfriend, you've got a head start. You live above a pub *and* you have a brother AND you'll soon be going to a mixed school. All I've got is a sister, a school that might as well be a convent, and a dad in a useless job. Well he might enjoy helping old ladies with their shopping trolleys, but what chance have I got of meeting anyone rich and famous on a bus?

What I'm getting at is that I don't think it should be like you said, with a flat prize of a fiver no matter *who* wins. Seeing as I've got all these handicaps and you've got all these advantages, I think we should have different odds on winning, like dogs do. So – if you're the first you should win at two-to-one, i.e. get two quid from me. But if I'm the first I should come in at five-to-one, i.e. get five quid off you.

I hope you think this arrangement is fair. I think it is.
Today I miss you more than ever.

luv,

Max

PS   In case your Maths is as bad as ever, this assumes
our stake's a quid.

Hornsey
London N8

August 28th

Dear Jean,

What do you mean, I'm not being FAIR??!! I was
going to increase the odds in my favour even more,
seeing as I'm fatter than you. But then being the kind
person I am I thought it wouldn't be nice to bankrupt a
friend. Fat chance I've got of that, being ten stone four.

So all right, it's probably my own fault that you're
eight stone and I'm not. So all right, I'm probably weak
willed and pathetic and eat too many chocolate bars.
BUT – it is not my fault if my dad's a bus conductor
while yours is a publican. Pubs are good for meeting
boys. On the buses, all a girl can meet are old people
and the unemployed. Those are well-known Facts.

It's bad enough you leaving me to cope with
Haringey Girls on my own. Denying your advantages
now you're going mixed is just about the last straw.

Two quid if you win, four quid if I do. That's my
final offer.

Max

Yours sincerely,

Max

96 Sheraton Road
Hornsey
London N8

Sept 2nd

Dearest Jean,

Ta ever so much for your phone call. You're right, it's crazy to argue when we go back so far. Half a lifetime is a long time – seven years!

At your request I am writing now to officially confirm the terms we agreed yesterday on the telephone. Two-to-one on you winning, three-to- one on me, seems fair enough now that you remind me that at five feet seven I am three inches taller than you. It is true as you so kindly point out that many boys today prefer a taller girl (e.g. Prince Charles), or one they can properly get hold of (e.g. Prince Andrew). So perhaps I am not as handicapped as I thought.

Now that I come to think of it, you are quite a short sort of person.

Hoping this finds you on top of the world (geddit?!).

kind regards,

Maxine

PS   Guess what?! Do you remember Keith Edwards, the guy from Hornsey High with the dead sexy walk? Well, he was on a bus today and saw me in the street and WAVED!!!! Well, sort of made a V-sign really, but Imelda up the road said that definitely means a boy is *interested*. Hornsey High have already started back, so guess what bus stop *I'll* be hanging around tomorrow at four o'clock??!!

The most boring place in the world
Hornsey
London N8

Sept 3rd

Dear Jean,

I know it's not my turn to write but I'll drop dead of boredom if I don't do something. If I don't die of Pneumonia first, that is.

Today I hung around the bus stop outside Hornsey High for TWO HOURS and all that earned me was a soaking. No Keith Edwards, just two hours of Hornsey rain. I'd spent hours getting ready, as well. I looked dead good, too – I'd got on Sue's black plastic jacket and that pencil-line skirt of hers that makes me look almost thin. I bust the zip but I put it back into her wardrobe before she got in from work so maybe she won't notice. I don't fancy getting beaten up by her when it was all for nothing.

God, Hornsey must be the most boring stupid place in the world. We're so far from the middle of London I might as well live up in Lancs with you. Not that Ashton-under-Lyne sounds like anything to write home about. But I'm glad you did – if only so I know I don't

5

have to bother getting jealous. God knows why your parents had to move you 203 miles away just so you could live beside a load of demolition sites and closed-down mills. Sue's new boyfriend Derek is a travelling salesman, and he says A-u-L is the kind of place they make television documentaries about. I don't think he meant that as a compliment. Still, as your dad says, it's good for trade that Ashton's got the highest proportion of pubs of any town in Britain. I suppose people up there drink to forget.

When I came in today, I asked Mum for a swig of her sherry to warm me up, but she just swiped me one. I was only looking for sympathy, but she's hard as nails, that one.

Yours, sneezing a lot,

Maxie

PS Now I feel guilty for slagging off Mum. She's just come into my room and said that she's taken the afternoon off work on Friday so she can buy me a new uniform. AND she reckons she should have enough to buy me a non-official super-sexy PENCIL-LINE SKIRT!!!! She's been saving her tips for me all summer. She is sweet.

Sheraton Slums

Sept 6th

Dear Jean

Well – it was awful. The new-school-uniform expedition, I mean. Dead embarrassing. AND I still look like a rubbish tip.

Mum was in her overalls when I met her outside the shop. Bert had only given her two hours off after all so she reckoned she didn't have time to change. Well, can you imagine going into a dead posh shop like Banhams The School Outfitters with your mum in purple nylon? AND she reeked of frying fat and vinegar. I could have died. Seeing as that wasn't on, I just kind of slithered away from Mum and pretended she wasn't with me.

Everything I looked at, though, Mum pounced on and went 'Ooh' and 'Aah' and 'Oh Dear' and said ever so loud, 'Haven't the prices gone up?!' I was supposed to get A WHOLE NEW OUTFIT. In the end all I got was two new blouses, a sports shirt, and two pairs of cotton bum-warmers. Who wears *those*?! All the other girls are in mini-briefs now. I'll get laughed off the trampoline.

The saleslady tried to flog us a new skirt but Mum gave one of her daft laughs and said she could take my hem down another couple of inches. Waste not want not, giggle stupid giggle. Huh. She'll laugh on the other side of her face when I'm had up for indecent exposure.

But the worst was when I took the stuff to the cash desk and the woman whispered, 'And will Madam be paying by *voucher*?' Vouchers – ?! You know, like we were so dead poor we were on the dole or something. Luckily Mum didn't hear, she was still too busy bargain hunting on the knicker counter. She'd have been ever so hurt. It was for her sake really that I decided to put that snotty woman down.

You'd have been proud of me. I put on my best posh voice and snarled that of course we weren't on vouchers. 'You know what rich people are like,' I said, pointing at Mum, 'dead eccentric.'

Well, I could tell that put the saleslady in her place but two seconds later when I turned round to yell at my rich eccentric mum to come and pay, you'll never guess who I found standing right behind me. Muck-Mouth

Michelle, all brown from Majorca and with her arms FULL of new clothes. From the smirk she gave me, she'd obviously heard every word. Oh Christ. How am I ever going to face her at school on Monday? It'll be all over the place now that I'm not just Dead Common, but a liar too.

No, I am not looking forward to the new term, especially without you. Don't take it personally, but you were the only other dead common girl smart enough to be in the top stream. Do you think I'd fit in better in Ashton-under-Lyne?

Max

PS   What do you mean, you want to know more about 'that girl Imelda'? There's nothing to tell. Her name's Imelda Maloney. She lives up the road, her parents are Irish, she's got about a million brothers and sisters, and she fancies Bob Geldof. I hardly know her really.

96 Sheraton Road

Sept 10th

Dear Jean,

Well, the first day of term was typical. My sweet big sister Sue got the day off to a good start by kicking my leg in for borrowing her skirt. Then Bat-Face shouted at me cos I was limping so much I was late. Then Muck-Mouth Michelle made everyone laugh by saying probably I was late cos I'd come on my Rich Eccentric dad's bus. Huh – so what if the number 14's never on time? I'm *proud* my dad makes time for all the old people to get on. If Michelle's dad was on the buses, he'd probably leave them to get run over.

Otherwise, the day was quite unremarkable.

You should see my leg where Sue kicked it – it's not just bruised it's *dented*. She pretends to be so sophisticated because she's seventeen and works in a boutique, but really she's a yobbo. She's just jealous because it's me that's the brains of the family. Still, I suppose it could be worse, I suppose I could have a brother like you. But don't you listen to Bob – you've got a lovely nose. At least Bob the Dog lets you hang around the football club and get an eyeful of his mates. That one with the short shorts (?!) *does* sound a bit of all right!

Not that I envy you having to pretend you're interested in football. I agree with Mum. She says football's just a load of sweaty men chasing a bit of leather. Well, that's what she always yells at Dad when he's slumped in front of *Match of the Day* and she wants to catch up on the news. You know my mum, even if Dad reckons he's Hornsey's answer to Arthur Scargill, it's her who really worries about The State of the World. She wrote another letter to Mrs Thatcher today, mother-to-mother, about the price of school uniforms and having Problem Children who beat each other up. I suppose she was thinking of Mrs Thatcher's Mark, he's always getting into trouble.

Anyway, enough from me, it's time to get my beauty sleep (har har).

luv

Max

PS   I told a lie, there was one good thing happened at school today. In French, Hairy Henri asked who wanted a penfriend in France, and gave us a list of names to choose from. No one else was that bothered, but I found a *Jean* on the list, so have written to her. I like Jeans, they are much nicer types than Michelles.

London
The South of England

Sept 17th

Dearest Jean,

I'm sorry you're still sick as a pig about living in Ashton-under-Lyne. I've been thinking deeply about it and have decided that you'll just have to do like my mum always says and Look on the Bright Side. Ashton-under-Lyne's got to have one. Have you tried the graveyards? An old town like that's bound to have some dead interesting dead people. Every time I pass a graveyard now I really miss you. I'll never forget how much you cried that time in Highgate Cemetery. I know my stupid dad only took us there so we could sing 'The Red Flag' round Karl Marx's tomb, but it was sweet the way you got cut up about all the little dead babies instead. You're dead feeling, you are. Some day you'll make somebody a really great mother.

Oh, bugger, now I've made myself cry again. Children didn't last long in the olden days, did they? I hope I don't die young. Poor Mum, she'd be so upset. I don't want to be greedy, but I wouldn't mind making it to ninety-five or so. How about you?

Yours,

Max the Morbid

PS   I forgot to say – congratulations on rechristening
Ashton-under-Lyne as Ashton- under-SLIME. I'm
going to write that on the envelope. Write back as soon
as poss to tell me if it gets there!

96 Sheraton Road
Hornsey
London N8
The CAPITAL of England
Great Britain
The United Kingdom
Europe
The Northern Hemisphere
The World
The Solar System

By Return of Post
Sept 21st

Jean – (I cannot tell a lie and call you 'Dear')

What do you mean, I've offended your Northern
Pride? I didn't know you had any. It was you that called
it Ashton-under-Slime – you started it. Just because the
postman gave you a lecture about being proud of your
roots. And no I don't give a toss if he does look just like
Brian out of *Coronation Street*. I'm sure I wouldn't know
who Brian Tilsley is, we in the South only watch
EASTENDERS now.

Please also note that you have NOT won our bet, and
that I am NOT sending you £2 by Return of Post as
requested. Being told that you're pretty by a postman
does NOT count as having a REAL boyfriend.

I am deeply wounded by your cruel words. I am

NOT a Stuck-Up Southerner. I am – sorry, WAS – your best friend. Please find enclosed the card you gave me on my fourteenth birthday. As you will see, I have torn it up.

Yours,

M. Harrison (Miss)

96 Sheraton Rd

Sept 26th

Dear Jean,

You're right – we're both wallies. I was a right wally for tearing up your birthday card. You were a right wally for listening to your postman. Probably he was just trying to stir it. Fellas never like girls being friends, that is a well-known Fact.

Thank you for admitting that your postman's got bad breath. That was very honest of you, especially as it's lost you two quid. I mean, I know you'd never go out with anyone who smells, even if he *is* a dead ringer for Brian-beautiful-Tilsley.

Thank you too for returning my card. You have glued it back together again very nicely. Looking back, I can't believe I could be fourteen and still so childish. I think we should let sleeping dogs lie and pretend we never had this argument. You should know me better than to think I'd ever look down on you for having to live in the North of England. Of course I like living in the South, but it takes all sorts. Also your parents are originally from the Provinces so at least you're getting back to your Roots.

That's what I meant about looking on the bright side.
Ashton-under-Lyne is probably where you belong.
Even if it does take you miles away from me.

I miss yer

luv

Max

PS   No French letter's come for me yet. Still, I suppose
it'll take time for that French girl to write it. Writing to
her in French took me HOURS!

Londres

Oct 1st

Dearest Jean,

A pinch and a punch for the first of the month but
only little ones seeing as I'm so happy – guess what,
today I got MY VERY FIRST FRENCH LETTER!
And French Jean isn't a girl SHE'S A BOY!!!

It's like this. French Jean twigged I'd thought I was
writing to a girl, because I'd asked him things you only
ask another girl. Like, are you on a diet, and is your bust
big too? God, I'd never have told him about my
problems Up Top if I'd known he was a boy Jean not a
girl one.

Anyway, he was dead nice about it all and said I
shouldn't worry about having big boobs because he
REALLY LIKES BOSOMY GIRLS!!! I nearly died
when I read that – I mean, it was dead embarrassing, but
sort of made me want to faint, too. Anyway, he's
seventeen, and dead good looking, and clever AND

13

rich! He's very modest, though. He said it's just good luck he was born with so many advantages. You can imagine how long it took me to translate that mouthful! I think the only thing Jean isn't good at is languages. He wrote to me in French.

You'll never guess what his dad does – he's A BUSINESSMAN! Of course I didn't want to put him off, so I told him that my dad's the Head of London Transport. Well, that isn't a total lie – Dad *is* the Chief Shop Steward at his garage.

But the best thing about Jean is his name. I asked Madame Henri how you pronounce it, and it's just like the English say 'John', only all soft and squidgy like you've got a mouth full of gum. DEAD romantic! Of course stupid Sue tried to spoil it by telling me all the Frogs stink. She says that's because they're always eating frogs legs and garlic. But I just think she's jealous because no one'll ever send HER a French letter. She's so bad at French she still thinks it's funny to say 'Oui oui' when she wants to go to the toilet. Never mind. Tonight I'm so happy I could even forgive Sue for being related to me.

Gotta go – time for bed and (I hope) SWEET DREAMS! Do you think an English person can dream in French?

LOTSA luv,

Maxine

PS Saw Keith Edwards on the bus again, and he made a V-sign at Muck-Mouth Michelle instead of me. What did I ever see in that nerd? English boys are dead boring, that's what I always say.

Dear Jean,

I know I wrote yesterday but I've just got to get something off my chest. It's my dad, I've had it up to here with him.

Last night he was on late shift so I didn't get to show him my letter from Jean. So today when I got home from school I wanted to tell him my good news first thing. He was pottering about in the garden, so I opened the window and yelled out, 'Hey, Dad, I've just got a French letter – do you want to see it?' I thought he'd be chuffed, but instead he speared himself with the spade and told me to go wash out my rotten filthy mouth. Sue'd overheard and was giggling like mad but wouldn't tell me why. She said I was too young to understand. But I do understand, I know all about racism. I should have guessed Dad wouldn't be pleased I'd got a French letter – after all, he always says, 'Wogland begins at Calais'. For a so-called socialist, he isn't half prejudiced.

Then he stomped in and said I should be ashamed of myself, shouting things like that when the new neighbours were outside and could hear. But I'll bet the Cuthberts are more open minded than he'll ever be. I told Dad I didn't think they would care, and he got even madder and yelled, 'No. That Lot Probably Bloody Wouldn't.' Turns out he's even prejudiced against them just cos their names are Amanda and Nathan.

Then Sue and me got half an hour on how Hornsey was Going Down Hill, what with all the Nobs moving in. Dad does exaggerate. Just cos we're the last of the council houses before the private ones begin, he kept moaning, 'We're on the front line – that's what we are. You just wait – we'll end up hemmed in by the woolly hat brigade.' Nathan's got ban–the–bomb symbols on his. It's great, you'd never guess he's a teacher.

I just hope Nathan didn't cotton on to how racist Dad is. He probably thinks we're pig ignorant as it is, what with our garden being full of handicapped gnomes. Mum's so into Waste Not Want Not she can't even bring herself to throw away the one I decapitated practising for Wimbledon. Oh well. I suppose it's not all Dad's fault he's got a chip on his shoulder. He did have a rotton deprived childhood.

Huh – just like me really!

Yours,

Misunderstood, N8

96 Sheraton Rd
London N8

Oct 4th

Dear Jean,

Thank you for ringing. Yes I AM glad that you're not jealous about French Jean. I expect YOU'RE glad that I'm not jealous about Shorty Shorts. Even if I didn't *sound* glad, I'm very happy for you. It's nice that he walked you from the football field to the bus stop. And it's nice that when the bus came he said 'See you around'. I agree that sounds promising.

It's just that I still don't think that means I owe you £2. A boy has to take you somewhere special before you can call him a REAL boyfriend. A bus stop doesn't count. I think we should get this bet on a proper official footing. Put it this way. When and if Shorty Shorts or anyone else takes you on a real ROMANTIC date, please send me proof. Cinema tickets will do, or those takeaway things from McDonalds. Then and only then will I cough up.

It's not that I don't trust you – it's you that don't trust me. Why should I be jealous because that Sharon asked you home to hear her records? It must be very nice to have a friend in your class. Of course I wouldn't know any more. All the other girls in 4A know I remain loyal to you, so I sit on my own. In fact I'm not even jealous that your parents have bought you a dog. As you well know I've always wanted a dog, but Mum says it's not fair to keep one cooped up in a flat. I hope your dog doesn't become an alcoholic – that must be one of the hazards of keeping a dog in a pub.

Can't write any more, too depressed.

Max

A corner of the 'playground' (huh!)

Lunch hour
THE NEXT DAY
Oct 5th

Dearest Jean,

Please ignore my letter of yesterday, I take it all back. I might as well admit it, I'm sick to my stomach and that's not just the school dinners. The way I see it, you're bound to forget me now that you've got that Sharon AND your dog AND that fella with the short shorts. I am jealous.

I'm only writing this letter to you now because it's better than standing in the playground on my own. I can't tell you how lonely I am. And it's so HUMILIATING. Every time the bell rings and we change classrooms I want to die, because I don't know if anyone will want to sit next to me. Mostly I end up lumped with the other rejects in the class, e.g. with Rosie S., that everyone now calls Slag-Bag because she's supposed to have DONE it. Michelle and Suzanne say that once you've done it people can tell, it shows in your face. I've looked and looked at Rosie but I can't see any difference.

I can't believe that only three months ago you were by my side, laughing at Bat-Face. Well, today she got her own back. She'd made us write one of those boring essays: 'What I Did In My Summer Holidays'. This morning she finally got round to handing them back, and in front of everyone she had a real go at me.

I'd written a dead good story about how you and me went pony trekking in Epping Forest and you got knocked unconscious and lost your memory and only a tape recording of my voice brought you round. You'd have cried if you read it, it's really real. But Bat-Face wasn't impressed. She read out the saddest bits in a silly voice and made everyone laugh. Then she said, 'I know some teachers have praised you for your "vivid imagination", Maxine, but as far as I'm concerned you're a compulsive liar.'

Smarmy nosey git, with her Greek tan. What *did* she expect me to write about – 'My Seven Boring Bloody Weeks in Boring Bloody Hornsey'? All she really wants to know is how much money we've got. Sometimes I wish to god I wasn't brainy. Then I wouldn't be stuck in the top stream with all the Suntan Snobs. Being brainy I don't fit in at home either. Mum's OK, but Dad's always saying the sooner I leave school the better. He reckons I should learn about the Real World.

Sometimes Dad gets all soppy and says he's only against me getting educated because of Today's Economic Situation. He's scared that I'll end up with some daft phoney government job like throwing beer cans down a sewer so I can fish them out again. That's when he says that studying like mad'll only break my heart. Other times, Dad just says he's anti books because it's sitting around reading them that makes me fat. Sue says the same.

Well. I'd better end this letter before I make you want to end yourself. If you can think of ANYTHING to cheer me up, please write a.s.a.p.

I miss you. Terribly.

love,

Max

PS   I forgot to say Ta for ringing. I LOVE your new accent. You're beginning to sound just like someone out of *Coronation Street*.

Hornsey, N8

Oct 10th

Dear Jean,

Whoever said, 'A Friend In Need Is A Friend Indeed' must have been thinking of you. I was so touched by your letter that I even showed it to Mum. She was very impressed. She said that you sounded quite mature considering that you've always been such a bad influence on me. Anyway – I've been thinking about all your good advice, and you're quite right. It IS silly to think you can have only one friend in the world.

Actually I've got a confession to make. You remember that Irish girl Imelda, that lives up the road? I've been getting quite pally with her. I didn't like to tell you before, in case YOU got jealous (!??!) Now that we've decided to act mature, I can tell you confidentially that her full name's Imelda Mary Anne Maloney and she's a red-head. Knowing Imelda is very educational, seeing as the Irish are Catholics, just like the French. Imelda pointed out that I'll never properly understand Jean if I don't understand his religion too. So she's giving me a crash course.

Mostly though, Imelda talks about the Pope. She's dead keen on him. She's saving up so she can go to the Vatican and kiss his ring before he dies. He's quite old. I suppose she's a bit barmy really but she's kind of nice. And interesting. The RCs are dead romantic, they have incense and singing and flowers and dress up a lot. It's much better than all that boring Protestant stuff at school that not even the teachers believe in.

Anyway – got to go now, there's a French test tomorrow and I've got to revise. Speaking of which, I'm a bit put out that I haven't heard yet from *La Belle France* (The Beautiful France). Do you think Jean is worried by the age difference? I hope not. Personally I think I've grown up loads even since you and me last wrote, e.g., I used to be a jealous kind of person, but I'm not any more.

With kind regards to you, and to your friend Sharon.

Luv yer,

Maxie

Oct 11th

Dear Jean,

Praise the Holy Virgin Mary that we're not going to be jealous any more – today I got my second ever letter from Jean and with it he sent his photo and he's EVERY BIT AS GORGEOUS AS HE SAID HE WAS!

Honest to God, I swear I'll never call French people Frogs again. Jean doesn't look like a frog he looks like someone on the telly. Honest – he's got these enormous great big dark eyes. I go funny all over just looking at them. Also he's got lovely black curly hair, and he's dead tanned. That's from all the skiing he does, water skiing in summer, snow skiing in winter.

Mum thinks Jean's lovely too, but all Dad said was, 'Huh – typical bloody Dago, if you ask me.' I felt really hurt for Jean. When I looked at his photo again I could see his lips quiver. As for those lips – WELL!!! Let's just say that he's got a FULL MOUTH. I think that's called SENSUOUS.

Sorry – I just can't write any more. I've gone all faint. It must be today's netball. I'd better give in, and go to bed.

Amicalement votre

(That's 'yours amicably' – what Jean wrote on the back of his pic. Isn't that ELEGANT!?!)

Maxine

xxxxxxxx

xxxxxxxx

Dear J,

HELP! I'm scribbling this postcard on the bus. I've worked out what Jean's on about now. HE WANTS A PHOTO OF *ME*!!! But I just *can't* send him one. If he sees how fat I am he'll never call me his Small English Friend again.

What'll I do? Please ring me AS SOON AS YOU GET THIS CARD. I'd ring you, but you know how hard it is to get my dad to unlock the phone. Even if the flat was burning he'd leg it to the fire station rather than clock up another 10p to British-Bloody-Privatised-Telecom.

Do not forsake me.

Yours,

Max

Fatsville

October 15th

Dear Jean,

Thanx a trillion for your phone call and good advice but I'm so weak with hunger I can hardly hold my pen. This cottage cheese and lemon rind diet is really awful.

I've been exercising too, like you said. Imelda took me tonight to a Dance-In at her church youth club and I danced non stop for two hours. I was ten stone three pounds six ounces when I left home, and ten stone three pounds *seven* sodding ounces when I crawled back.

Sue says it's all the lemonade. Imelda says I should be so lucky as to be fat. Mum says lemons cost the earth so I'd better find a cheaper diet, sharpish. So now I feel guilty as hell, as well as fat.

Now Dad's just barged in and told me to Turn That Bloody Dirge Off. I've been listening to Prince's 'Purple Rain' while I've been writing. I've only played the title track ten times. Anyway, you'd think Dad'd start to like it by now. It's ever so good, it's really sad. Just because he's on earlies tomorrow. He's got no feelings, that's his trouble.

Sue hasn't, either. I'm practically bald, she pulled out loads of my hair just because I borrowed her jumper. You know, the green one with the pom-poms on the shoulder. It was just right for the Dance-In, cos you look at those wobbling, instead of my boobs. I told Sue that, and all she did was yank out some more of my hair. She says I've made her jumper sweaty. She is entirely lacking in Christian charity.

I hope Jean isn't. I hope he believed me when I said all the family portraits and photos were stolen along with the silver. I hope you're right, and I can lose two stone in a month or so and then get a beautiful picture of me taken.

But I've got a nasty feeling you're wrong.

Yours disconsolately,

Max

PS   *Half an hour later*

I've been thinking, and it's cheered me up. I'd been dreading the Dance-In, in case no one wanted to dance with me. But Imelda's big brother Frankie had me on the floor for hours. He says I'm a dead good mover, and that I've got a figure just like Fergie.

Well, I think that's a compliment, but Sue says that just means I'm a Lump. That girl's got no respect for royalty.

PPS   Frankie is sixteen and a half and quite tall and he's got lovely creamy skin and black hair and big blue eyes.

PPPS   But Imelda says he's only interested in greasy motorbikes. Anyway, he's got freckles – yuck!

Sheraton Rd

Oct 19th

Dear Jean,

I'm sorry about your mum and dad. Actually I was glad to hear your dad uses words like that too. I thought only mine did. You should hear him when he's stuck behind a lady driver. DEAD embarrassing, especially if he's got the window down. Dogs have feelings too. It's rotten your dad calling Patch that, just because he pees all over the place.

I am glad you like the sound of Jean. And he's BIG! I've worked out what 184 centimetres means in English – it's six foot one inch!! That's even taller than Frankie. I do like size in a boy.

Poor old Princess Di. Fancy having to pretend she likes flatties. No one's fooled. I bet when she's on her own in the Palace she struts around in heels all the time. Although maybe I should save my pity for myself. I asked Dad for some new shoes the other night and he said if the Royals weren't so well heeled *I* could be. That meant no. It's getting so that I'm ashamed to show my feet anywhere. The shoes I've got now used to have heels but I've worn them so much they're like slippers. Honestly – I wouldn't exaggerate.

Gotta run. It's ten p.m. and I've still fifty sit-ups to do before bed.

Yours sincerely,

Maxine

96 rue Sheraton
Londres du Nord
(North London)

Oct 26th

Dearest Jean,

AU SECOURS! (Help!) I've had another letter from Jean and he's more or less *demanded* a photo of me. He wasn't horrible about it, he said he was very sorry about the family silver, but he can't keep writing to a girl when he doesn't know what she looks like. I know what he means. I've got his photo stuck right inside my French dictionary. It's very inspiring, the times I don't know what I'm on about.

What this is leading up to is my BRILLIANT idea. Why don't you send me YOUR photo so I can send it to Jean and pass you off as me? Just temporarily, I mean. Until I've lost a couple of stone. Seeing as you're so gorgeous. I know flattery gets you nowhere but even Sue once said you're not bad looking for a friend of mine.

Of course please feel free to think this request over in your own good time. Meanwhile I am enclosing 80p in stamps, to pay for the photo booth. I shall be grateful to you until the day I die.

Yours gratefully,

Max

96 Sheraton Rd
London N8

Oct 28th

Dear Jean,

Further to your phone call. I am touched that you're worried about me getting myself into trouble, but please don't let that stop you sending me the photo.

Anyway, I've been thinking, and you're wrong. Apart from me being fatter, we look *ever* so alike. Especially if you don't wear your glasses. And if you blow-dry your fringe the way I do mine. I've looked it up in Sue's beauty book, and if you hold the brush tight you CAN get rid of curls. As for your nose, that's a minor problem. Just bend your head in the photo booth, Jean'll never notice that you haven't got one. Aside from these things, we're almost identical. I mean, we've both got shortish brown hair and biggish brown eyes. Don't you remember how we used to tell everyone we're sisters?

If you ask me, I look a sight more like you than Sue or even Mum and Dad. It beats me how two skinnymalinks like them produced a big bruiser like me. Sue says that too. I think she's right, I probably am adopted. She always says that when we row. Now that I think of it, I *could* be your mum's kid. I mean, you're lots older than me – nearly ten months. It would have been hard for her to help run the pub with two small babies, as well as Bob the Dog, so I wouldn't blame her for giving me away. Wouldn't it be great if we really are sisters!!!

What I'm getting at is that you've nothing to worry about, so please PLEASE send me your photo now. For your convenience, I have enclosed a stamped addressed envelope.

Yours faithfully,

Maxine (could–be–Oglethorpe) Harrison

PS   You've got cheek bones and I haven't so don't wear any blusher. If you puff your cheeks out a bit, that will be even better.

96 Sheraton Road

November 1st

8 am

Dear Jean

Just a postcard to say THANKS A TRILLION for sending the photo. You look dead good in it, just like me. But better, of course.

I promise to write back the minute I hear from Jean!

Yours in eternal gratitude,

Maxine

Dear Jean,

Well, I haven't heard from Jean yet but I thought I
should write tonight because I'm feeling philosophical.
For starters I thought I should be nicer to my friends, so
perhaps you'd like to know what I want for Christmas.
There are only thirty-nine shopping days left and I
wouldn't want you to get into a flap. Personally I think
Musk perfume is dead sexy. But believe me, anything
will do. After all, Christmas is God's birthday, not
mine.

In case you haven't noticed, I've gone very spiritual
since this morning. It's all Imelda's doing. She's been
drumming it into me that SOUL matters more than
THINGS. Apparently, today's the day the Catholics
pray for the dead, so Imelda got me to have a go at it. I
was down on my knees in front of this home-made altar
thing her mum has at home. Then I told Imelda all
about the dead people in my family. It was really sad,
we both cried. Then we played some records. It was
really good, we cried some more. Then we got on to
politics. That was awful, I don't understand *anything*.

What beats me is why life gets to people different
ways. Dad says it's because of all those foster homes he
was in that he's such a socialist. Mum says it's because
her mum worked herself into an early grave after her
dad scarpered that *she's* a Tory. I don't know. Mum says
only women can run anything, a home or a country.
That's why, when the papers are slagging off Mrs T,
she always writes to her, to cheer her up.

I asked Imelda her opinion, and she reckons she might be a women's libber too. She wants to be the first woman Pope. She's got a good chance, she's very holy. I'm quite holy nowadays too, but when I was praying for all my dead relatives tonight I still felt cross with Mum and Dad. I think they were really mean, getting married without a grandparent for me and Sue between them. I know we weren't born then, but they could have thought of us.

At Christmas the only relative we get presents from is Mum's sister Sal who's in the army. She's very nice but absent-minded. She keeps sending us the same ashtray saying, 'Greetings From the Third Tank Regiment, West Berlin'.

You're all right, now you're up North you've got your ageing nan and all your cousins and things just round the corner. You'll probably get loads of Musk and leggings for Christmas. Imelda's got so many relatives it isn't fair. She's even got a nice mum. Mrs Maloney's just like a real mum, one in the adverts. She's always cooking and dishing up and asking if you've had enough. My mum thinks she's done us proud if she dumps some cold leftovers from the chip shop on the table.

Oh well. I shouldn't be too hard on Mum and Dad, they had a rotten childhood. I'm just glad they've got me, to cheer them up. Sue too of course, even if she's not as sensitive as me. I asked her tonight if she'd prayed for the dead and she said she was too busy getting ready to go out and whoop it up with Derek. You ought to see Derek, Sue's posey travelling salesman. Or maybe I should say smell him. Me, I wouldn't buy anything from a fella who's had a bath in Brut. I wish I didn't have to share a room with her. I have to listen to her droning on about him all the time.

Time to sign off. I've loads more prayers for the Dead. Maybe I'll be extra kind and say one for Derek.

He can't help it if he's English.

Yours philosophically,

Maxine

Dear Jean,

Sorry for the long delay in writing but Bonfire Night
and collecting for the Guy kept me busy. Of course I am
too old for such things but someone had to supervise the
small Maloneys when they were out collecting. Me and
Imelda made £5. The small Maloneys made 50p. It was
fun really.

As usual the grown-ups were against everything.
Mum was against us collecting for the Guy because she
says it's begging. Dad was against the whole thing
because he says Guy Fawkes was the only man who ever
entered parliament with honest intentions. Mr and Mrs
Maloney said it was Against Religion to burn the Guy
because the real one was a Catholic.

Mum and Dad and the Maloneys were so busy
arguing about terrorism that no one noticed when
Frankie started lighting fireworks outside. No one, of
course, except our new neighbours, the Cuthberts, the
ones around the corner. They poked their heads over
the fence where their garden joins ours and gave us a
lecture about blowing our heads off. They're real
teacher types – I can see now what Dad means about
Hornsey going downhill.

Then the Cuthberts overheard the row about

terrorism and said How Frightfully Interesting and joined in. I expect they think us lot in council houses only talk about stuff on the telly. The next thing, one of the grown-ups produced a bottle and the whole caboodle was half-cut. Honest to God, we could have burned down half of Hornsey and no one would have noticed. Don't grown-ups make you sick, always going on about being responsible then getting drunk in charge of kids?

Actually, I could have been seriously injured. I singed my fingers saving one of the smaller Cuthberts from eating a sparkler. It had never been allowed to have one before. They're deprived kids.

Frankie was great. He grabbed my fingers and stuck them in a jar of orange juice. He said that'd cool me down. Then he went bright red. It's a shame he's only interested in motorbikes.

All for now. We've got a netball match against Wood Green Comprehensive on Saturday, so I need all the sleep I can get.

Yours in training,

Max

PS   Yes I did get picked! At last! I'm goal defender!

Dear Jean,

I'm so miserable it isn't true. It's been two weeks and I still haven't heard from Jean. He must have hated the photograph. No offence, but maybe Bob the Dog's right about your nose.

And I buggered up the match against Wood Green Comprehensive. We were ten–nil down by halftime and Miss V. said I was the worst goal defender she'd ever seen and took me off the team. But Kim who replaced me wasn't much better. We still lost ten–nil. It was all the fault of those stupid workmen. There was a gang of them watching from some scaffolding. Every time I jumped to stop a goal they yelled out things about my boobs. So I tried to jump in a way that didn't make them wobble. If you're a 36DD, that isn't easy.

I'm sorry you're miserable too. It's getting really serious about your dog. It isn't his fault he got so frightened on Bonfire Night that he peed into the beer. Your mum's cruel, thinking she can stop Patch by rubbing his nose in it. Do you think that's how she toilet-trained you? That's probably why you've got such a turned-up nose. Even if the rest of you is quite pretty.

Anyway, I hope that this letter has at least cheered you up. I hope so, cos I luv yer.

luv,

Max

Dearest Jean,

'Scuse the wobbly handwriting but I'm scribbling this on the bus to school because I've just got to tell you! I've finally heard from Jean and he LOVES THE PHOTO! Really! He's gone bananas! He's even stopped calling me 'vous' – he's now on to 'tu'. That's the French way of saying 'thou', remember. It's what Madame calls the INTIMATE form!??!

Can't write any more, nearly there. But thanks a TRILLION again.

Much love,

Maxine

PS   I've asked Mum to call me 'thou' too.

96 Sheraton Road
Hornsey N8

Nov 24th

Dear Jean,

What does your stupid brother mean, we've got to be a pair of lezzies just because I said something about loving you? He's got no right reading your letters, you've got to find a better hiding place. Any dope (no offence) would think of looking under your mattress.

I've found a great place for yours, I keep them rolled up inside my wellies. Your letters are in the right welly,

Jean's are in the left. If it rains I'll have to find another
hiding place but down here in the South it's been very
dry lately.

You can tell your stupid brother from me that it's not
true you can only *like* a friend. The French don't even
have a different word for 'to like' and 'to love' – it's all
aimer to them. I suppose that will go above Bob the
Dog's ignorant head though.

I've stopped showing your letters to the girls at
school. Michelle and Kim started saying things a bit like
your brother. It's them that started everyone calling
Rosie a 'Slag-Bag'. They spread stories about everyone.
The other day Rosie started crying when we were
paired for Chemistry and told me that she HASN'T
done IT. All that happened is that once she got snogging
with Keith Edwards at a party. Then when she
wouldn't go any further he told everyone he HAD done
it, just to spite her. (You remember Keith Edwards, he's
the one from Hornsey High who walks about with his
legs apart, like he's got a cat stuck inside his trousers.)

I've shown the girls Jean's photo. Even Michelle said
he was dead good looking, so I guess he must be. But I
already knew that. The real reason I show them Jean's
things is to stop them saying I'm 'not normal'. So yes, I
do know what it's like, but I don't think it's a good idea
to go out with Shorty Shorts just to get your brother off
your back. You know that Shorty Shorts calls girls
names like *that* too, and Mum says that if a boy talks
about *any* girl like that, you can be sure he'll talk the
same way about you if he gets the chance. Maybe you
could try telling your brother that secretly you've got a
boy at school. Just don't lie to me, that's all! Even for
the sake of winning our bet!

Mum says that friends should always be honest and
respect each other's secrets. She should know – on
Friday nights when Linda's round you'd think there was
a Cabinet meeting going on in the kitchen. I'm not even

allowed in for a crispbread. Mum says that me overhearing her and Linda talk would put me off marriage.

I don't think that Linda ever sells anything from those catalogues of hers, it's just that humping them around gives her and Mum and all the other women a great excuse to gas. Well, that's what Dad says. But maybe he's just jealous because he doesn't really have any friends of his own. I am glad I've got you.

Much LOVE
(and SOD YOU TOO, BOB, if you're reading this!)

Maxine

Londres N8

Nov 30th

Dear Jean,

You're never going to believe this! Jean wants me to come to France! Well, what he actually said was he hopes we can meet up 'very, VERY soon'. I think that means he's saving up for my ticket. Jean says he'll let me know more about his plans for the holidays in his next letter. I can't wait. Christmas in Paris, here I come!

I asked Dad if he could help out with the costs and he said, 'I should cocoa'. I think that means he will, if I work on him. I mean, I've never been on an educational trip, and meeting Jean would be VERY educational (know what I mean?!?!).

I guess I should also get on with some saving of my own. At the moment most of my pocket money goes on saccharin. But I'm not doing bad – I can now nearly get into a *size fourteen*!! Well, a big size fourteen. But it still leaves me skint. So, I have decided to do as Dad says and get a job. I reckon that if I can save £13 a week, it will take me three weeks to save up the hovercraft fare to France. Just in case Jean loses the ticket, I mean.

And if I LOSE ten pounds a week, it will take me only three weeks to get into size tens. Then I can take Sue's clothes to Paris with me.

I haven't asked Sue yet, but I'm sure she'll agree. The French are dead keen on fashion, so it would be a good advert for her boutique. A famous designer might even stop me in the street and ask me where I got my clothes. It would really put it on the map if I could say, 'Ravers, Hornsey'! Sue would probably get a commission. I'd let her keep half of it. Soon I'll be rolling in money. Tomorrow I'm going down Wood Green shopping centre to get a Saturday job.

I promise not to forget you when I'm rich.

beaucoup d'amour
(lotsa luv)

Maxine

Hornsey

Dec 1st

Dear Jean,

I'm writing so soon because I need your help. I've found out the hard way that getting a job is just as hard as the Labour Party says it is.

It's all very well Dad believing in child labour but the law's against it nowadays. I asked in all the big shops,

Marks and Sparks, BHS, but they said they can't legally take anyone on until they're fifteen years three months. I told them I was very mature for my age, but they just said 'come back in another ten months though, we'll probably be full up then too.' That's when I decided to go down-market and try Woolies. I mean, I couldn't be worse than those rude girls who snarl, 'If it's not on the counter we haven't got it'.

But Woolies has standards too. I'd cottoned on by then about the age thing so I told the lady that I was already fifteen and a half. She just gave me a funny look, saying she'd have to see my birth certificate. I went as red as a fire engine at that. (It's horrible this blushing. I read in the paper that it's teenage hormones that does it. They give you spots too.) Anyway – once I'd got over going red I told the Woolies lady that I couldn't show her my birth certificate seeing as it was lost at sea when my family moved here from France. I pretend a lot nowadays to be French, it's really useful.

I put on my best French accent, and pointed out that with French being my mother tongue I'd be a real asset. I'd be able to help with the tourists and everything. I could see the lady was very impressed, she became dead friendly and even started laughing. But she still told me to come back only when I'd got a copy of my birth certificate, and then she'd see what she could do. Thanks for nothing! If I wait till I'm 15 yrs 3 mths to earn some money and go to France, Jean will have found someone else and gone off me.

So – I need your help re getting a job. Unemployment's supposed to be worse up North, but that can't be true – you've got a job cutting up sandwiches for your mum and dad's pub. That's given me an idea. Do you think if I tell them you're my best friend, the new managers of the Hornsey Tavern might give *me* a job?

It would help a lot if you could write a reference. Just

say things like you've known me since we were eight and that I already know where the crisps are kept and that I'm very honest. That should swing it. Thanks ever so. It's really useful having connections.

Yours gratefully,

Maxine

Hornsey

Dec 4th

Dear Jean,

You really are A Friend In Need, ringing me the minute you got my letter. But maybe you ought to watch it. My dad swiped me once just for *getting* a phone call at Peak Time. He says it's an act of Class Betrayal, financing holidays abroad for British Telecom shareholders.

No, I don't hold it against you that you can't give me a reference. It's not your fault that your dad's breaking the law, employing you to make sandwiches. I was really shocked to learn that *someone I know* is a criminal.

It's terrible, the amount of crime nowadays. I took your advice and asked Mum if I could get a paper round, but she said that with all the perverts loose on the streets I'd end up being *in* the papers, not delivering them. I said I didn't think perverts get up at five am, but Dad said I couldn't hold down a job that means getting up so early anyway. He says I'm so hard to get out of my pit in the morning that I should have been christened the Horizontal Champ.

All that leaves is baby-sitting. I've done like you said

and put an ad in the newsagents, so keep your fingers crossed for me. I'll give you a ten per cent agent's fee if I strike gold.

luv,

Maxine

PS   I've just kissed Jean's photo goodnight and nearly fainted. God, when I think about IT I could die, it's so exciting. Woops – DON'T let Bob read this! Perhaps we should have a code for talking about IT. Any ideas?

Dear Jean,

I know it's not my turn to write but I've got to tell SOMEBODY. No I'm not dead or ill or anything but I wish I was. Seriously!

You remember the ad I put in Mr Habib's? Well, I've had two replies so far and they had nothing to do with baby-sitting. They were OBSCENE.

The first call was from a man who said what he really wanted was a model. He said I wasn't to worry about posing in the nude (?!) because he lives in Highgate and that's where all the Real Artists live. I gave him a dead good answer, I said Highgate was too far for me to travel. Then I slammed the phone down. He'd asked my bust measurements, and everything.

The second call was from a man who hardly said anything at first. I kept asking him how old his children were and he kept humming and hawing and in the end he said his wife had left him and taken the children with her and what he really wanted me for was SOMETHING ELSE. Well, when I finally worked out what *that* was I really gave him a mouthful. I told him that my dad would smash his face in if he ever rang back again. In the end the man started crying and said he was sorry and rang off but he still left me feeling – you know, kind of *dirty*.

I wish I could tell Mum and Dad but you know what they're like. Dad'd probably say it was *my* fault for putting in the ad. Dad clocks me one if I'm in after nine as it is. He says that's 'asking for trouble'. If he knew I'd had dirty phone calls he'd probably not just have a lock on the phone but electric wiring. To electrocute me if I went near it, I mean.

Dad always says that All Men are Beasts, then Mum mutters that It Takes One To Know One. I expect she'd be more sympathetic if I told her about the calls but she'd get into such a state it's not worth it. Every time there's something on the telly about a rape or a child murder she starts to cry, then shouts at Dad about why doesn't his Silly Old Union campaign about something serious for a change. Dad yells back that it does, but that it's 'her friend' Mrs Thatcher that's making travel unsafe by axeing people like him, train guards and bus conductors.

All I want is a cuddle, not another argument.

Two hours later

Now I've written to you I don't feel so bad. Also Sue came in and saw I was crying and was really nice. She said they'd had a couple of obscene phone calls at work, so now they keep a whistle by the phone. Sue says that you don't give them the satisfaction of listening, you just shout YOU USELESS PERV! and then blast their ears off. We had quite a giggle, practising.

Mr Habib was nice too. I went down to the shop to take out the advert and though I didn't say why, I think he guessed. My eyes were like balloons. He mumbled something about the British being a Strange Lot, and gave me a big tube of Smarties that had passed its Sell By date. He knows they're my favourites. Now I've eaten them all and am probably two stone heavier as well as still unemployed.

Oh, well. That's enough moaning from me. I may be poor but so was Jesus. Imelda says there's a Higher Purpose to everything, so if I'm not going to get the money to go to France maybe it's because God's got other plans for me. Maybe he wants me to do good and be a nun. I'd really suit being a nun, they mostly wear black and it's very slimming.

What do you think is the Higher Purpose of obscene phone calls?

I miss you very much.

luv,

Maxine Marie Harrison

(Marie is the name I've decided to get if I'm Confirmed, like Imelda. Marie is the French for Mary. Then my whole name would sound French, except for Harrison.)

PS   A miracle! Mum's just told me that the Cuthberts round the corner want me to baby-sit at the weekend. Mum is sweet – it turns out she's been asking everyone for me. Sorry, but now I'll have to give her the ten per cent agent's fee.

Dec 9th, 10 pm

Dear J,

I had to write and tell you straight away. Baby-sitting is AWFUL! I thought the kids would go straight to bed and I'd be able to watch the telly in peace, but I've only just got the little sods upstairs. And there isn't even a telly here! Can you believe it??!! Amanda and Nathan (that's their parents) reckon that telly warps people's minds. And tonight it's *Dallas*!

The kids are dead stuck up, too. They told me off for calling them Seb and Al instead of posey old Sebastian and Alexandra. They didn't care WHAT I called them when I was teaching them what a firework was. But tonight they even told me off for calling them 'kids'. They said that's Degrading To Children. They should try Little Sods for size. They're only six and seven but they talk dead posh too, just like their parents. Amanda told me that *I* sound like someone out of *Eastenders*. I've been thinking about that. How come she knows about *Eastenders*, when they haven't got a telly?

Their flat's gorgeous though, it's just like Alexis's in *Dynasty* but a bit smaller. There's hanging plants hanging everywhere, and white sofas with no tea stains on them. You wouldn't believe it's just round the corner from Sheraton Road.

Gotta run, that's Blake and Krystle at the door.

luv,

Max

Dear Jean,

Treat this as a warning. Guess what I got paid for baby-sitting? An AVOCADO!!?? One stupid sodding avocado. My advice to you – never sit on *anyone's* babies without making a contract first.

Mum's raving. She says that proves what she's always said, that the rich only get rich by being so bloody mean. She says they've all got short arms and long pockets. Dad agreed, then asked how could Mum still vote Tory.

Amanda's line was that it's Good for the Generations to Mingle. I think that means me being stuck for nothing with her sods. I was there five hours as well, because her meeting ran into overtime. It was about the 'Cultural Deprivation of the Working Class'. What about me having to do without *Dallas*?

You'd have thought it was the crown jewels, the way Amanda handed me that avocado. She said it was full of vitamins. She told me not to peel it first. She must think I'm stupid or something. I know what an avocado is, we did one in Domestic Science.

Dad was dead nice, he was on my side for once. He got all sentimental about me being only fourteen and already Exploited. Mum gave him some of her sherry and then he sang 'The Red Flag'. Even Sue said we should demonstrate outside the Cuthberts'. Dad said he'd love to, but that this government's so anti-worker that they've probably even made it illegal to picket your neighbours.

That sent Mum off. She'd had a lovely letter from 'That Woman's' secretary only this morning, and she waved Downing Street's writing paper in Dad's face

and said he'd drunk quite enough. She's worried that
with all the political rows in our house me and Sue'll
end up being disturbed children. I must say I do feel
disturbed tonight. I think I might become a socialist as
well as a Catholic. Imelda is taking me to Christmas
Mass.

Yours fraternally,

CHILD LABOURER

PS   I found out how Amanda knows about *Eastenders*.
Turns out she's a lecturer in Cultural and
Communication Studies, whatever that is. Anyway, she
says she can't criticise things unless she watches them
first. So she watches videos of all the telly progs up at
her college. What a hypocrite!!!
  I wouldn't mind a job like that. Fancy getting paid to
watch *Dallas*. I didn't watch *Dallas* OR get paid.

luv,

Max

c/o 1 Sheraton Avenue
Hornsey N8

Dec 16th, 10.30 pm

Dear Comrade,

  All right call me a mug but I'm back next door.
Before I came over Dad taught me how to put in a pay
demand in a proper Union-like way. But I don't think I
dare. Anyway, I've thought up my own strategy.
  I'm going to tell Amanda and Nathan, subtly like,

that I'm saving up for a *book*. Not any book in particular just *a* book. You know, like I've never had a book of my own before. They've got books all over the place here, they'll probably feel so dead sorry for me they'll even pay me extra.

I'll let you know later how I get on.

Yours in struggle,

Max

Later

Amanda gave me 50p and an old copy of *New Society*. I'm too depressed to carry on living. By the time I've saved enough to get to France Jean will be dead anyway. And that's just the good news. When I got in Mum handed me a letter from Jean that she'd forgotten had come (how could she??!!). I could have been depressed a whole six hours earlier. Because no, even if Jean did pay for me we couldn't meet at Christmas. His rotten parents are forcing him to go skiing in the Alps instead.

Jean's really cross with his mum and dad. They say the exercise is good for him. Har! *I* could have helped him to exercise (?!). They get all the luck. The only winter sport we get in Hornsey is scraping damp spots off the wall.

Now I'm going to cry myself to sleep.

love,

Max

Dearest Jean,

Tonight I feel full of the Christmas Spirit so I should
post some of it to you. Even Kim and Michelle were full
of Good Will today and didn't tell everyone that I only
got ten cards in the school's Christmas post. Only six of
them were from me to me, so really I did quite well.

Ta ever so for your prezzie, which arrived today. I
love surprises so I haven't looked, just had a bit of a feel
and a sniff. You know I like Musk so I don't suppose it
really is one of those plastic bubble bath things from
Marks. I do hope you like your present from me. It's
only small but remember the best things in life come in
small packages (e.g. your nose).

Nothing's come from Jean yet, but it's early days isn't
it?

I feel very Spiritual tonight – I've been out singing
carols with Imelda and Frankie. Their youth club
organised a Live Crib outside Hornsey Town Hall. It
was fantastic – Imelda was the Virgin Mary, and there
was a real live donkey and a real live baby Jesus. It was
all Frankie's doing. He borrowed the donkey from that
inner city farm place, and got Jesus from his Mum.

Catholics are always raising money for sick children
and things. They're dead good, really *caring*. You
should have heard the mouthful Frankie gave anyone
who didn't cough up. Talking of coughing, I've gone
hoarse from all my singing. I'd better put my little weak
bod to bed.

Have a Happy and very Holy Christmas. I wish you

were here, at this time of year (I'm a poet *and* I know it!). Even if you are a Protestant.

Much love,

Maxie

Hornsey

Christ's Mass Day
(Dec 25th)
1 am

My dear little sister in Christ,

Don't get upset but I've gone Catholic. Properly, I mean. As soon as the holidays are over I'm going to get myself signed up to become a real one. It's the Midnight Mass that did it. It was great.

I'm just back from church now. I can't sleep, I'm so excited thinking about all the presents I'll get tomorrow, and God. All is Right in My World. Even Mum and Dad were having a bit of a cuddle on the sofa when I got in. Dad's dead chuffed because he's got this Christmas off. As he said, some other poor sod can deal with the drunks.

I felt a bit guilty at that seeing as I was a bit tiddly myself (?!). Don't tell anyone but before the Mass, Imelda and Frankie took me into The Three Brewers. MY FIRST TIME IN A PUB! (Sorry, sitting upstairs from the Hornsey Tavern with you and a bag of crisps doesn't count. This time I was a customer!) Imelda said I could pass for eighteen when I'm all dressed up so I was very brave and got Frankie to get me a cider.

I got it! So did Imelda. We were quite giggly by the

47

time we got to St Joseph's. I hope we weren't too much trouble on the bus. We sang 'We Three Kings' at the tops of our voices. The altar boys were singing pop songs. They'd all been in The Three Brewers too.

The altar boys are GREAT! One of them thought I was SEVENTEEN!!??!! I'd got on my favourite jumper, Sue's green one with the pom- poms. I felt very grown-up and spiritual. I'm now down to nine stone ten pounds and NO OUNCES!

As for that foreigner who's got the same name as you, the less said about HIM the better. I haven't had a thing from France, not a present, not even a card. I sent him *his* present way back in November.

Still, I suppose there is a Higher Purpose to my broken heart. It was after all my love for Jean that brought me to Catholicism. That's the One True Faith, you know. Please don't take that personally, even though you are a Prod.

I am praying to Saint Paul for your conversion.

luv,

Maxine

LONDRES

Christ's birthday plus two
(December 27th)

Dear Jean,

Please tear up the last letter I sent you. In the event of your death I don't want ANYONE reading the cruel things I said about Jean. His beautiful present arrived today and I feel so happy, and ashamed.

It's an Advent Calendar. Seeing as it's now nearly January I ate all the chocolates inside it at once. I was back up to nine stone twelve this morning but I DON'T CARE. When you've been starving for love as long as I have, who counts calories?

I will from tomorrow though. Jean's inspired me by SMOTHERING the top of the calendar in kisses (!). I've told Mum that in future I'm not even allowed second helpings of Christmas cake.

Now all I have to do is wait for his Christmas card.

Much love from your best friend after the best Christmas I've ever had,

Maxine

PS   I'm also enclosing the letter I wrote to you last night. It's so dead miserable I wasn't going to send it, but you can ignore that now.

Christmas Day in the Workhouse
Hornsey

(Dec 26th) 10 pm

Dear Jean,

I'm right cheesed off – all I got for Christmas was an ashtray, school clothes, an LP and a jumper.

The LP is Duran Duran's DREADFUL 'Arena'. Mum doesn't seem to have remembered me telling her that I don't like Duran Duran any more. I'd cried when I told her, but obviously my tears went in one ear and out the other, the way she says everything does with me. I pretended to be pleased but I was very hurt. Mum and I used to be close, more like sisters, just like in the ads.

49

Now there's a real gulf between us. She even shouted at me because I let the brussel sprouts get soggy.

Thank you for the bubble bath. It's just what I wanted.

That's more than I can say for Sue's present. She gave me a man's razor. Sue says it's just as good as a ladies' one, but I know for a fact that she got it discount off Derek. He's a rep for Remingtons. I don't shave my legs anyway. Sue says I should, otherwise she'll be too ashamed to identify my body if I get run over.

Derek gave Sue some Musk. When the pair of them were in the room together you almost needed a gas mask. I'm glad nobody gave me Musk, it's dead tarty.

Imelda also gave me some bubble bath.

Hoping you had a lovely Christmas too,

luv,

Max

PS   I suppose I shouldn't be too hard on Mum. Dad's main present to *her* was a SLEEVE IRONING BOARD!?! Men – I'm off them totally. Jesus is the only one that's ever understood me.

LONDRES

New Year's Day
(January 1st)

Dear Jean,

Yesterday I finally got Jean's Christmas letter and in it he says he thinks it would be VERY INTERESTING to have a FOREIGN WIFE!!??!! Isn't it funny. I think

English boys are boring and he thinks French girls are. We've got so much in common. Face it Jean, he's more or less asked me to marry him. YOU OWE ME THREE QUID!

Anyway our New Year party was GREAT! Everyone came – even a cousin of the Maloneys who's on holiday from the Missions. Just imagine, a priest – in OUR house! And I was so happy that Rosie and Anna said I was totally different from at school. I was a bit nervous about asking them to the party, in case Mum and Dad showed me up, but they were really well behaved.

Mum put some kitchen knives down on the floor and did her pretend Scottish sword dance. Dad hummed 'Scotland the Brave' with his fingers over his nostrils so he could be the bagpipes. I was getting all ready to be embarrassed then I saw that Rosie and Anna were cracking up so I had a good laugh too.

The only thing Anna didn't like was getting Amanda and Nathan's sympathy vote. Because she's black they droned on and on about How Difficult life must be for her. She told them that actually she was an African millionaire's daughter. That shut them up. They don't approve of millionaires.

The food was really brilliant. Bert brought pies from the chip shop, Mrs Maloney made some soda bread specially, and Amanda brought a bean salad that no one touched. The only sour note was the German sausage sent by Aunt Sal. Mum was dead proud but no one knew what to do with it. Then someone worked out you had to peel off the skin. Then someone else (they were all well bottled by then) giggled that it looked just like a French letter. I chimed in about the one I'd just got that morning and everyone went quiet and then they all started laughing fit to bust.

It was Frankie who put me straight. No one else would tell me. I collared him in the hall and he ummed and aahed then said that 'French letter' is slang for something that Catholics aren't allowed to use. Like Protestant youth clubs? I said. Then Frankie coughed and took a deep breath and stared at his feet and told me the truth. And went bright red.

I don't blame him. So did I. Did you know that French letters is slang for *condoms*?!? Don't grown- ups make you sick with their dirty minds.

Mum and Dad are just coming round from their hangovers, so I'd better go and make a pot of tea. Apart from them having filthy minds, I quite love them really. And Jean. And you. And God. God I'm so lucky I could cry.

Your best friend,

Maxine (soon to be Gaultier?!) Harrison

Hornsey

Jan 5th

Dear Jean,

Ta ever so for the long letter listing all your New Year resolutions. They're much more realistic than mine. I'm sure you've got a good chance of starring in *Top of the Pops* by the end of the year. You are only eight stone.

You were dead honest telling me all of them. Especially the one about not doing NUMBER TEN until you're at least eighteen. The code you've thought up for IT is brilliant. I've pasted it inside the Catholic Catechism Imelda's given me, so that when I'm thinking about sinful things I'll remember where to look.

The only Resolution that I've kept so far is to tell anyone who offers me sweets that I've gone Diabetic. I've found it makes it much easier to be strong willed. I've told Mr Habib in the corner shop that he's never to sell me chocolate again, because even one Smartie sends me into a coma. Mr Habib was very sympathetic, he said that until further notice he'll only sell me fish fingers.

I'm going to tell the girls at school that the Diabetes came on sudden over Christmas. I expect they'll feel ever so sorry for me. Especially when they learn that Jean's just asked can he marry me. I'll seem quite tragic really.

By the way, you didn't mention Jean's marriage proposal. Haven't you got that letter from me yet? I was expecting to find £3 in yours. I'm not cross, but I expect it in the next post.

> lotsa luv,
>
> Maxine

> 96 Sheraton Road
> Hornsey
> London N8
>
> January 9th
> 9 pm

Dear Jean,

Further to your phone call of January 7th, I have as you suggested thought the matter over, and reluctantly decided that I will accept your terms. For the purposes of our bet, Jean will only count as a REAL boyfriend after we meet in the flesh, and have our first kiss.

I think you drive a hard bargain, but then I've always said you've a right hard side. It must be the Northerner in you.

We Southerners aren't spineless either, so I'm going to lay down some new conditions too. YOU only get to say you've got a *real* boyfriend after a minimum of three dates. Real ones, remember, to somewhere *special*.

As for your comments about me going 'all religious and weird' — what can I say? I was ready to give you a right earful on the phone but then the line went dead. I suppose your dad yanked you off it. It's your own fault. I did warn you. You ought only to ring when the pub's busy and your dad hasn't got time to run upstairs and check on you.

Oh dear. I hope your dad didn't thump you. Now I feel really worried. I'll just stop for a minute and say a prayer for you to St Jude. He's the Patron Saint of Hopeless Causes. Then I'll get back to this nonsense about me being a religious maniac.

Two prayers later

(Just to be on the safe side I asked the Virgin Mary to intervene on your behalf, too.)

Look, it's like this. I've not become a Catholic, I'm only THINKING about it. Dad says you shouldn't sign up for anything without reading the small print, so I've been giving the Vatican the old one-two. I've been finding out exactly what Catholicism would expect of me.

It was only after the French letter/German sausage business at the New Year's party that I realised Catholics aren't supposed to use THINGS (contraceptives). That means Catholics who do IT can end up having a baby every year. Imelda said if Jean and

I get married at sixteen, like I plan, I could have thirty-four children by the time I'm fifty. And that's not counting for twins!! I don't even like children, so that's put me off a bit.

Hoping this has set your mind at rest,

Maxine Marie Harrison

Hornsey

January 12th

Dear Jean,

Sorry, but no deal. That Bill from the Football Club didn't ring you for a whole two weeks. Obviously he wasn't sitting at home polishing his football all that time. Obviously he was two- timing you with someone else. You know as well as I do that it's pathetic to claim that bumping into him on the football field counts as a third date. You hang around it all the time. I'm surprised at you, haven't you got any PRIDE? I wouldn't make myself obvious like that, it's cheap. Maybe we should drop this whole bet. It's not worth the rows. God knows we need each other.

No, I haven't enjoyed the beginning of term. The first day I swanned in all excited, because of Jean. I started talking about the Chunnel Tunnel, saying how great it would be for Anglo-French marriages when you could get from London to Paris in just three hours forty minutes. You could have Sunday lunch with one lot of in-laws, then pop over to the other lot for your tea. I thought that was bound to get the girls dying to know how far things have gone between Jean and me. But Michelle spoiled it by barging in with her racism again.

She said she'd flood the Chunnel when it opens. She said the Frogs would use it to send us all their rabid rabies. We had quite a fight. You would have been proud of me. This time Michelle didn't manage to pull out any of my hair.

The other rotten thing at school was that Michelle's side-kick Kim saw straight through my story about being Diabetic. She got everyone laughing at me. All through break they kept saying, 'Come on, Fatso, have a sweet!' Then in the canteen they bought yummy things like ice cream and chips and ate them in front of me, licking their lips.

It's all right for them, they're like you, they've got hollow legs. While they were drooling over calories, I had to toy with a lettuce leaf. Michelle made everyone laugh even more by saying that the salads in our school are so limp they should be served on crutches instead of on plates. She's right, my lettuce had definitely had a very hard life, but I had to pretend I loved every soggy mouthful. It was really humiliating.

Imelda says that I shouldn't let the likes of Michelle and Kim get to me. She says that only insecure people put themselves up by putting other people down. She's very mature is Imelda. She says that comes from being the eldest girl in a big family. She said she would pray for Michelle and Kim but I've asked her to pray for me instead.

All for now. Happy New Year again.

luv,

Max

Dearest Jean,

SWOON! Great news! JEAN IS COMING TO
LONDON! For a week! Seven whole days! In April!
When Spring is in the air ...????!!!!????!! No time to write
more. I only just got his letter and am scribbling this
before (YUCK) school. I can hardly see straight, I'm so
excited!

Ton amie mieux
(your best friend)

Madame Maxine Jean Gaultier

Later (8 pm)

I've just had an emergency religious consultation with
Imelda. She says that some Catholics DO practise birth
control. The not-so-strict ones, I mean. I wonder how I
can find out if Jean is one of them?

Don't get me wrong – I'm not thinking of doing IT
when he's here. I just thought it would be interesting to
know. For my general knowledge, I mean.

luv,

Max

PS   Even if I don't want thirty-four babies, maybe I
wouldn't mind having ten or so. Fancy being able to say
to the man you love, 'Hail, I have borne thee a child'!,
every other year! Doesn't that just send shivers up your
spine??!!

PPS   I've just realised that the school holidays in France might be different to ours. What will I do??? I can't be at school every day when Jean's here. HELP!

Hornsey

Jan 15th

11 pm

Dear Jean,

I'm SO miserable. I'm fat, I don't look anything like your photo, and our house is so horrible I'll die of shame if Jean ever sees it.

Buying a new house is dead easy nowadays, it says so on all the adverts, but Mum and Dad won't hear of it. Mum says that if this house was good enough for her mum to die in it's good enough for her to live in. AND she says that we haven't got enough money to buy. That's a lie. I know that for a fact. If she can splash out on Spanish Gut Rot for her Friday nights with Linda, she could easily save up for a house.

I don't even know where I'm going to put Jean. Mum won't let him stay, even if we do move to a nicer house. She says with a boy under her roof the only way to stop me Getting Into Trouble would be for her to sit up on guard all night. I told her she's got a filthy mind and she hit me. I hate her.

Even you're against me. I could have looked more like your photo if you hadn't worn blusher. I told you not to – what price friendship, eh? Sue says that pretty girls often pick plain or fat girls for their best friends. That's so that when they're out together the boys notice the pretty one more.

Thinking about it I now see our entire friendship differently. No wonder you 'liked' me!

So long,

Max

Dearest Jean,

Please PLEASE ignore the letter I sent you this morning. I knew during History that I shouldn't have done it. We were doing Elizabeth the First and all the people who plotted against her and suddenly I realised that's what Sue is. Just a plotter. A stupid stirrer. She's just jealous because she doesn't have a best friend. She's dropped everyone for the sake of that travelling salesman of hers. But you and me have been friends since we were eight and I was thin then. So that can't be the reason you like me. I'M SO SORRY!! PLEASE FORGIVE ME!!

I bunked off Maths to go to the Post Office and get your letter back but the post had already been collected. I went to the main office and asked if I could go into the sorting room to find it. I said I'd accidentally posted Mum's Child Benefit book and that we were so poor we'd starve without it. I looked pathetic, I was genuinely crying, but they still said rules were rules.

I was late for Biology then because I'd ruined my mascara and had to scrub it off. It's not the waterproof kind, I can't afford it. I only came back to school because I've already had one detention this week. But Hairy Henri caught me coming out of the loos and now I've got another.

I'm not trying to make you feel sorry for me. I don't deserve it. You can hate me if you want. It will probably do me good to feel even more lonely than I do.

I know you are the best friend a girl could ever have. Please let me know a.s.a.p. if you will have me back.

Yours, apologetic from the bottom of my stupid heart,

Mad Max

Hornsey

Jan 20th

To:
Miss Jean Oglethorpe
THE BEST FRIEND A GIRL COULD EVER HAVE
Ashton-under-Lyne

Dearest Jean,

Thank you from the bottom of my heart for forgiving me. After your phone call yesterday I cried for hours. You are such a good person I know you will go straight to Heaven.

I've said a prayer for you tonight. It's to help you get more than two out of ten next time you have a French exam. Then when you're as fluent as me we can pretend that we're tourists when you next come to London. Being a French tourist is really good. I was one this evening. I didn't want to go home seeing as Mum's still not talking to me so I went down Wood Green, window shopping. Then this man started walking beside me muttering. I thought he was just another loony, but then he asked if I was wearing tights, or stockings. I gave a big shrug of my shoulders and said, 'Ai am not understandeen nusseen, perapps ze nice Ingleesh bobbeee over zhere can be 'elpeen you?'

Of course I didn't even know if there was a Bobbee Over Zhere but Perv-Face didn't either. So he just sort of shrivelled up under the drop-dead look I've been practising lately in the mirror, and belted for it. It was really GREAT. I bet I totally ruined his day.

After that there was no stopping me. I didn't just window shop I went inside too. You know how sniffy those boutiques are when they can tell you're broke? I mean, the snotty way they say 'Can I Help You Madam?' when what they really mean is 'Sod Off' ? Well this time instead of crawling away I said, with a very sweet smile, 'Sod off yourself '. Except I said it in French and they didn't understand. After that they left me alone even if they did mutter a bit about stupid foreigners who can't speak English.

The only time being French can't help you out is when you want to try on the clothes. In one boutique I found a lovely size fourteen dress that I was sure would fit but they'd only got one of those big cattle-barn places for trying things on. You know, where all the other girls look down their noses at you because your underwear's old and you can't do up the zips.

So – I had to be English then. I whispered to the assistant that I was too shy to change in public because I'd just had a big operation and was covered in bandages and scars. She was dead sympathetic and let me change in the broom cupboard. There wasn't even a light or a mirror in there but I'm sure the dress fitted OK, so as soon as I've got some more money I'm going back to buy it. It's GREAT.

Imelda is taking me somewhere at the weekend to see about some WORK so you never know, soon I might be a millionaire after all! Then I could put Jean up in a hotel.

much luv,

Maxine

London N8

Jan 25th

Dear Jean,

I'm glad my letter inspired you re the usefulness of learning French. Your letter inspired me to try harder at Physics. You're right, there is something dead sexy about leaning over a bunsen burner with a boy. I can just imagine you and that Pete experimenting together!!??!!

Mum says I'll have to try harder at science anyway if I'm going to be the first woman pilot of Concorde. Last week I only got three out of ten for Physics. But by the time I leave school and join British Airways it will all be done by computers. As pilot, I'll just have to flash my gold braid at nervy passengers to calm them down, and to work out which children look house-trained enough to be allowed up to play in the cockpit. It's a good job for a woman because your family are allowed to fly free, so I wouldn't have to leave them with a nanny. Mum says I live in a dream world, but she would.

Yes, Mum and me *are* talking again. I'm so relieved. I

hated hating her. We had a really good talk the other night, we stayed up till TWELVE. Mum said she didn't like having to be suspicious about Jean and me, but it would break her heart if I made the same mistake she did.

I do feel sorry for her. She says Dad's all right really, but that she's totally missed her chances. She wanted to be a top secretary but then she had to leave school at sixteen. Dad was the first boy she ever went out with. I reckon it's because Mum's a frustrated brainbox that she writes all those letters to people about the state of the world. She says she's brainy really, but working in a chip shop nobody believes that — not even me and Sue.

I felt dead guilty then so I said maybe she could go to college. She is thirty-five but they do take quite old people nowadays. Mum says she'd love to go but we need her wages too much for that. Anyway, she says life's ground all the confidence out of her. It was so sad we both cried and she became really sentimental. She said she was proud of me, that I'm the spitting image of her at fourteen, brains and all. She cuddled me and said that even when I'm a grown woman I'll always be her sweet baby and that I'm never to throw myself away.

I do love Mum, even if I am a battered child. She said she was sorry for hitting me and she never usually says sorry for anything. She even said she'd give me extra pocket money during the week Jean's here. She said she wouldn't do it usually but you're only young once and it is a *special occasion* after all.

I still think Mum's wrong though, about not letting Jean stay with us but I do understand her a bit better now. I feel very mature, generally. I look at the other girls in 4A who are still into Duran Duran and praise God for my tragic life. I know it's only because I've been forced to be older than my years that I'm not still a silly teeny-bopper too.

Me and Imelda start our new jobs tomorrow. Dad

says a day's hard graft'll kill me, so I'd better grab some kip in case it's my last chance.

Yours in Maturity,

Maxine

The Factory
Sheraton Road
London N8

Jan 26th

Dear Jean,

I am now a Working Woman. Me and Imelda are HOME-WORKERS. Have you ever looked inside the top of a perfume bottle and noticed the little circle of cork that stops the perfume evaporating? Well, it's the likes of me and Imelda (CHILD LABOURERS, Dad says) that puts it there.

Today we wheeled Imelda's Mum's pram to this man's house and he gave us two big boxes of perfume bottle tops, a smaller box of cork things, two metal prodders each, and a tub of glue.

It's like this. You stick your first prodder in the glue then prod it into the bottle top so that the inside gets all gluey. Then you pick up a little circle of cork with your fingers and balance it on the opening to the bottle top. Then you take your other prodder and shove the cork as far as it will go, till it hits the glue and sticks. Hey presto, you've got one bottle top finished, and are on your way to your first million quid.

Apparently factories often farm out work to people like this man. Then they farm it out to women and girls.

That's because we're much better than men at delicate, fiddly jobs, and we like working at home, he says. I don't know why Dad's singing 'The Red Flag' again. It's money for old rope really, we're going to get £1.50 for every twelve gross we do. In case you've already gone metric up North, a gross is 144. Once me and Imelda have got our speed up (we only managed about half a gross tonight, i.e. 1/24th of £1.50), we'll be rolling in it.

We watch telly while we're On Shift and that's more than I can do when baby-sitting. Imelda and I have planned our Shifts around what's on telly every night. Stuffing corks isn't so bad when you can watch *Dynasty* while you're doing it. Me and Imelda are taking it in turns to be Boss. She was Boss tonight and gave us a tea-break during the second half of *Dynasty*. Alexis was REALLY disgusting and we wanted to watch it properly without getting glue on the sofa.

Sue wants to go to sleep now and says she'll beat me up if I don't turn the light off this minute. When I'm a millionaire I'll have a room of my own and then she'll be sorry. I bet she'll be dead lonely without me.

luv,

Max

PS   Imelda says that all this arm exercise is good for our busts. I'm a bit worried, though, that our right ones might get bigger than our left ones. What do you think?

96 Sheraton Road
Hornsey
London N8

Feb 3rd

Dear Jean,

Guess what? I'm going to Paris instead of Jean
coming here! Mum says that if I can save half the fare by
Easter, she'll chip in the other half. She's opened a Post
Office savings account for me, so that I can learn to
budget, and every week she's going to bank her tips.
People don't tip much in the sit-down part of a chippie,
but she reckons that if she gives people bigger helpings
on the sly, she should make enough to see me right. She
said even Mrs Thatcher would steal the odd chip or two
if it would help her children.

Mum's faith in the upper classes is amazing. She even
said, seeing as Jean's dad is a businessman, she's sure she
can trust his parents to see there's no hanky panky
between Jean and me. Now all I have to do is wait for
Jean's reply, telling me when I should arrive. I'm sure he
won't mind the change in plans. I've told him that the
mosquitoes in Hornsey are very bad at that time of year.

Paris in the springtime, here I come!

buckets of love,

Max

Dear Jean,

GREAT NEWS! Being a factory worker has paid off in more ways than one – Amanda is now paying me better wages too! She asked me to baby-sit tonight but I was VERY sniffy and said no, thank you, I've got a better paying job. She asked me how much I was getting and so now she's paying me £1.50 as well.

Actually she's paying me more than she knows cos I sneaked the bottle tops over with me and got the Little Sods to stuff them. They did at least half a gross between them and it totally knocked them out – it's only eight-thirty and they're in bed already. I didn't even have to read them Peter Rabbit.

I wonder what Jean would make of me being a Working Woman. He's dead romantic. He says that his wife shouldn't have to go out to work, she should have an easy life and only look after him and his children and the home. Dead traditional. I told Mum, and she sniggered that ALL wives are Working Wives it's just that some don't get paid for it. God she's cynical.

I think Jean's got a point. If a man really loves you he doesn't want you to stink of a chip shop like Mum. He wants the whole world to know that *he* can take care of you. Mum says that even if she does smell of chips at least she gets to see people. She says that being at home on her own all day used to drive her batty. She's got no romance in her. If I was at home all day I'd have more time to think about my husband.

Amanda and Nathan are due back any minute so I'd better clear up. I'll need to flush the vegetable curry she left us down the toilet. It looked so yucky I gave the poor little sods hundreds and thousands in sandwiches instead. Sugar's got loads more energy than boiled cucumbers. I'm surprised at Amanda, being a teacher she ought to know the importance of a healthy diet.

xxx

Max

Dear Jean,

This morning I got Jean's reply and he's worried about a girl my age travelling all the way to France alone. He's just like Dad. To hear him, you'd think I shouldn't be allowed out of the house except in a Securicor van. Jean says that anything could happen on a hovercraft. Like what? I've known about not taking sweeties from strangers since I could crawl. Since I've gone Diabetic I don't even take them from friends.

Jean thinks he should be the one to put himself out. So he's suggesting we stick to the original plan – i.e. he'll come to stay in our Hornsey *château*. The worst thing is, Mum says I should be *grateful* Jean's so protective. I think it's just an excuse so he can have all the fun of travelling.

I love Jean from the bottom of my heart but I'd fight him on this one if I had a chance of winning. But I don't – Mum told me Dad hit the roof when she said she was sending me to France. The same old story – how I'd get robbed or murdered if I travelled more than five miles from home. If you ask me, Dad's in more danger of those things when he's collecting tickets on the number 14 bus. The truth is, he's MEAN.

Still, I'd rather be with Jean in London than not at all so I'll just have to bow down to fate, I suppose. I don't know how I'll break it to him that he's got to stay in a hotel. Mum says I should tell him NOW, because he'll need to book in advance. But I can't. Not yet. There's still a chance she might come round if I work on her. With the estates they're building nowadays you can pay and have the key to your new front door within a month. It says so in the brochures I've put by her bedside. If I help pack, we could still be out of here by Easter. I don't rate my chances, though.

The REALLY awful thing is that Jean hasn't even sent me a Valentine card. How am I going to face them in school tomorrow? Michelle's already got two.

Yours miserably,

Maxine

Hornsey

St Valentine's Day
(Feb 14th)

Dear Jean,

It was good of you to phone. No, I don't really mind that you got three Valentines. You only told me that when I pushed you. I know I sounded angry but I swear to God we had a crossed line. It wasn't me who said 'You don't need to sound so smarmy'.

I hope you and Bunsen Burner Pete will be very happy. You're right, the pink card must be from him. Pink is the colour litmus paper goes in experiments. It was dead clever of you to work that out. When you leave school you should be a policewoman. If you don't get to be a rock star I mean. No offence, but Miss Piggy's the only TV star I know with no nose.

All I can say is thank God I've got Imelda. I couldn't have got through today without her. She didn't get any Valentines either but she says that's because GOOD Catholics don't believe in him. St Valentine I mean. He used to be a First Division saint but the last Pope demoted him. Being a saint is like the Football League, one minute you're First Division the next you've been booted down to Fourth and no one wants to light candles to you any more.

I explained that to the girls at school but Kim was still sarky, saying the French just boast about being great lovers. I said they didn't need to *prove* how romantic they are, it's them that invented French kissing. Kim didn't have an answer so she shut up. I hadn't planned that line, it just popped into my head. God must have put it there – Imelda was praying all day for me while she was at school. I'm sure God gets sick of Kim's sarkiness too.

Tonight Imelda and me did Over Time to take our minds off things. We stuffed TRILLIONS of bottle tops. If we can't be loved we might as well be rich, ha bloody ha. We could have done even more but Imelda was Boss and kept making us stop to say prayers to St Jude. You remember him, he's the Patron Saint of Hopeless Causes.

I'm knackered so I've got to go now. I just wanted you to know that I really DON'T mind your getting three Valentines. Did one of them smell? It might have been sent from your postman.

Yours sincerely,

Maxine

Dearest Jean,

Well, nine days have gone by, the longest ever
without me writing to you. I've taken so long to
respond to your apology because I had to think. Your
letter really made me cry.

I had no idea you were still so lonely up in the North.
I had no idea you had no one else to share your joy at
getting three Valentines. When you put it like that, I feel
honoured.

What is this nonsense about me saying you 'sounded
smarmy'? I wouldn't put it like that. You were just a bit
insensitive, that's all. Nine days is a long time – you
have suffered quite enough. I agree it's awful that the
Valentines turned out to be from your mum, dad and
dog. But at least your family think of you. Mine don't.
That's what makes me so sensitive. And Hormones.
I've still got them, how about you? Stupid question,
judging by the tear stains on your letter. Or was that
Patch?

And what a meanie your brother is, telling you who
sent the Valentines just because you kicked him. I'd
thump him too, for saying what he did about your nose.
Bob's just jealous because you've got all the brains in the
family. It's the same with me and Sue, but Bob's
probably extra jealous because he's a boy. Sue cheers
herself up by saying it's cute for a girl to be a little bit
helpless. Actually she's not as dopey as she makes out,
she just acts like she's had a lobotomy when Derek's
around.

God, I hope Jean doesn't expect *me* to act stupid. It's
bad enough that he's coming in seven weeks' time and I
still don't know where to put him.

Well, this isn't much of a cheer-up letter so I'd better

sign off. I think you're great even if Bunsen Burner Pete doesn't.

Lots of love from your best friend,

Max

PS I've been thinking. What if I don't like kissing??? I heard one of the girls at school say it's just like having a slug in your mouth.

Londres

March 1st

Ma chère Jean (my dear Jean),

I've just had the most wonderful letter from France. Jean's so excited about coming to London and finally meeting me that I've decided to stop feeling sick with nerves and get excited too.

We're going to have a GREAT time, I just know it. Jean wants to go everywhere. He's enclosed a long list – Madame Tussauds, The Tower of London, Buckingham Palace, the King's Road, Oxford Street, Regent's Street, Carnaby Street etcetera. The trouble is, I don't know where half those places are. And Mum never even lets me up Oxford Street on my own. She's got it into her head that drug pushers jump out of doorways and stick needles into your arm to get you hooked (HONESTLY!). She'd be better off worrying about the stuff that changes hands down at The Three Brewers. She'd never let me go to the toilet on my own if she knew what a den of vice Hornsey really is.

ANYWAY, the good thing about Jean wanting to do

London in style is that I've finally worked out how to sell the hotel idea to him. If he camped out here in Hornsey he'd spend half his holiday on the buses, trying to get to where the action is. So I've just written saying he'd be better off staying up town.

I'm a bit obsessed with money at the moment. The *bad* thing about Jean wanting to do the town is what it's going to cost. I've only earned twenty quid from the bottle tops so far and most of that went on that new dress. Do you think I should let Jean pay for me sometimes? Mum's always said that if you let a boy pay your way he'll expect to get *his* way in return. Other times she says that if a boy doesn't pay for you that proves he's trying to get you on the cheap. It's very confusing.

I asked Mum about what the hotel and the sightseeing's going to cost, but she says that if Jean's any normal kind of boy he'll be quite happy getting a cheap B & B near here and sticking around Hornsey. SHE NEEDS HER BRAIN SEEING TO!! No one comes to London to see Hornsey. Especially not the French. They're very sophisticated.

lotsa luv,

Max

Dear Jean

GREAT NEWS! Today I hit NINE STONE SEVEN for the first time in YEARS! Mum says I look like Pam in Dallas. I'll be happy if I can look like your photo.

I've been practising with make-up tonight. I've worked out that if I wear lots of blusher and shader I'll look like I've got cheek bones, too – especially if I suck my cheeks in. It's a bit hard to suck in your cheeks and talk at the same time, but when Jean arrives who's gonna be interested in conversation?! Roll on Easter!

Ta very much for your advice on when to go Dutch or pay your own way. You're a right women's libber you are, on the sly. But it's not surprising – I was shocked to hear that Bob even gets more pocket money than you. Why is his job clearing empties for your dad worth more than yours making sandwiches? Just because he's a boy. That sly bugger probably drinks whatever's left in the glasses anyway. Huh!

All for now. Mainly I just wanted to share the good news about my weight. It's wonderful not having to worry any more about what I eat.

luv,

Max the Minuscule

PS   How many calories are in an orange?

PPS   Have I *really* reached my Ideal Weight? All the tables I've read allow ten pounds either way depending on whether you're light or heavy boned. I've always thought I was heavy boned, but maybe that's cheating. How can I weigh them to be sure?

March 14th

Dear Jean,

What am I going to do? I'm skint and I haven't got ANYTHING to wear when Jean comes. Mum says she'll lend me her clothes but I'd look a right berk in floral nylon. Poor old thing, she think she's dead modern too.

I'm skint because I'm back in the ranks of the Unemployed. Yesterday me and Imelda finished another load of bottle tops and they turned out to be our last. Our boss said there's no more work for us, and paid us off. And we didn't even get any Redundancy Money. Dad was right about us being paid peanuts but at least it was something. I've still got the Post Office account Mum started for me but she says I break into that on the threat of death. It's so I can have a summer holiday, either a return visit to Jean in France, or a week up in Lancashire with you. (You're the booby prize.)

Only joking! If Mum gets enough tips and I find another job, maybe I could do both. I can't really be on the scrap–heap at only fourteen.

Yours,

Redundant, N8

PS Guess what?! I've just had a phone call from Michelle inviting me to her party! Maybe she's decided to be nice to me from now on. It's a bit last minute (it's eight already) but Mum says I can, so I'll go.

Dear Jean,

It's one a.m. and I'm writing this straight after THE PARTY. It was such a giggle I have to tell someone. Imelda would be shocked but I know you won't be.

Well, it seems Michelle didn't invite me because all of a sudden she LIKES me. Being such a brain-box I worked out that she just needed a load of girls to come cos she's got three brothers. All their mates were there, and she hadn't provided enough Talent. She also rounded up Rosie that she calls Slag-Bag, and Anna and Grace that she's always calling darkies. She calls *me* Snot the Swot nowadays.

Well, after a while Michelle started in on Anna and Grace. You know, calling them names. Anna took her shoes off and was all for stabbing Michelle with her stiletto but Grace stopped her. She's a Baptist and told Anna she should turn the other cheek instead of cutting Michelle's. I thought that was a bit wet myself even if I am nearly a Catholic.

Then someone turned the lights off and everyone started snogging. I didn't want to, so I went upstairs for a look around. Guess what I found in Michelle's bedroom? Anna and Grace, tossing all of Michelle's clothes OUT OF THE WINDOW!!!

It was that ever-so-holy Grace's idea. It's dead rainy tonight and she reckons that by the time Michelle's scrubbed the mud out of her clothes she'll have learned to keep a good Christian tongue in her head. She and Anna were giggling so loudly I had to keep guard. It was great. There were bras and knickers and skirts and socks flying all over Hornsey.

Michelle will never know who did it. Everyone downstairs was out of their brains. You should have seen the place. There were people spewing up everywhere. I counted two broken chairs and one broken banister and I left before eleven.

Now I see why Mum says I can't have a party here without her being in the house. I'm not even sure why I go to parties. I always have to wear the same thing, that old 'new' dress. I get all excited thinking I'll meet someone special who hasn't seen me in it before, but I always end up in the kitchen talking with the other girls.

Sue says I'm daft talking to girls at parties but I think it's better than snogging with someone you don't really like. Sue says I would get off with someone I liked if I made more of an effort to hide my brains from boys, but I said you can't hang your brains up with your coat. I thought that was a real clever answer.

I did neck a bit with someone at the party, though. I thought he looked sensitive as well as good looking. But then he started to snog with someone else straight after so he can't be. I felt dead tacky. From now on I don't think I'll even *think* of kissing anyone until we've had a PROPER DATE and I'm sure he likes me and I like him. I'd also like to be sure he won't KISS AND TELL. Keith Edwards was going round telling all the boys who he'd 'Done It To' before he'd even taken his jacket off.

Mum said something really funny. I didn't tell her anything about the party when I came in, but she must have guessed because suddenly she gave me a cuddle and said, 'Cheer up, love, you've got to kiss a lot of toads before you meet Prince Charming.' She is a sweet old thing sometimes.

Enough from me. I can hear Sue clumping up the stairs to bed so she'll want the light off. I need my beauty sleep too. I want to look my best when I see the state of Michelle on Monday morning!!

Hope you had a great Saturday night too,

luv,

Max

Dear Jean

Michelle *didn't* come to school looking like a rag-bag!
She looked like a teenage version of Alexis in *Dynasty*,
all claws and new clothes. God she makes me sick. It's
all right for her, she doesn't have to be a child labourer
like some of us I could mention. Now her dad's In
Computers (that's how she puts it, like the eejit lives
inside one), she gets more pocket money than ever
before.

Excuse the Irish ('eejit' is Gaelic for idiot) but it's St
Patrick's Day, and me and Anna have been round at
Imelda's. Mrs Maloney pinned some shamrock on us
and then when we left she warned us against getting
beaten up on our way home for looking Irish. Anna said
she was more likely to get hassle for being black but
Mrs M. said the English weren't too keen on the Irish
either.

So on the way to Anna's bus stop me and her
practised saying Piss Off in Rasta Gaelic. You say 'O
man you a rassclart gombeen eejit' and look fierce. No
one bothered us though except an old man who'd had
one too many and asked us if Our People knew His
People back in Kerry.

78

I wouldn't mind being Irish or West Indian. I don't know what's so special about being English, we don't even have a national costume.

At least Jean's looking forward to coming here. I got a nice letter from him saying he would like to stay in Claridges. He wants me to book him in, so I'm off on Saturday morning to ask at the travel agents.

Lotsa luv

Max

PS   Re our bet – I disagree. I'm glad Bunsen Burner Pete's finally seen the light and asked you out, but I don't think it's fair to eliminate me from the running when Jean's visit is now so close. I think the winner shouldn't be the first one to get three dates, but the first to get a marriage proposal. As Jean's only got to set the date, I'll probably win.

Fair dos? Let me know.

Hornsey

March 20th

Dearest Jean,

Today started awful and ended great. This morning I went to the travel agent but the girl REFUSED TO TAKE MY BOOKING! I pretended I was a secretary and said, 'I book my boss into Claridges all the time', but she told me to pull the other one and sod off.

Sue says it's something to do with my age. And my accent. And my clothes. I suppose it was stupid to go there in my school blazer, but I haven't got another jacket to wear since my boobs bust the zip on Sue's black plastic one.

I've written to Jean saying he'll have to find a hotel himself when he gets to London. It's probably for the best. I wouldn't even know if Claridges is the sort of place that's clean.

Sue says the French are very fussy about cleanliness. She told me about *bidets*. They're special bowls in their bathrooms for washing their feet in. She thought that was very funny. She says I must remember to ask Jean why they can't use the sink like everyone else.

Now for the GOOD news! When Jean comes I'm not going to look like an Oxfam shop reject after all. Thank God for catalogues!

Mum's friend Linda was over last night and accidentally left hers here. This morning after the travel agent business Mum found me flicking through it. I wasn't really putting it on, honest. I was just going 'Ooh' and 'Aah' and 'Look at those lovely clothes!' and sniffing and crying a bit. Suddenly Mum said, 'For God's sake, get out of that school blazer, I'm sick of the sight of it', and got on the phone to Linda and told her to sign me up for EIGHTY QUIDS' WORTH OF CLOTHES!!!! Great!

Mum says I've got to pay the first four weeks instalments myself, from my savings account, to show willing, but that somehow or other she'll find the rest. God I love her.

I'm too excited to write more. I've taken the catalogue to bed with me and now I'm trying to work out what to choose.

Much love,

Max

Dear Jean,

I heard so many opinions about what to get from the catalogue, that I didn't know *what* to choose in the end.

Mum said I should get something classic but Sue said that meant boring. Sue said I should get something trendy but Mum said that meant rubbish. Imelda said get something romantic but Frankie said that meant sexless. Frankie said get something low-cut but Mrs M. told him to go pray to Mary, Queen of the Virgins. Dad just said, 'Bugger it, look at the interest rates.'

Then Sue pointed out that if I didn't make my mind up pronto, Jean would arrive before the clothes do. They take four weeks to deliver and Jean's coming in four weeks one day and six hours (April 19th, 10.30 am).

I got in a real panic and now I've ended up making everyone happy except me. I ordered the navy blue cardi that Mum said wouldn't date, the orange lurex top that Frankie liked, the green and orange spotted trousers that Sue chose, and some white high heels with sparkly bows that Imelda said were dead feminine. Now I'm worried they won't all go together.

Amanda said I should have stuck to my own taste, but I've never had enough money to work out what that is.

Oh – and I got a black jacket of course, like everyone's wearing. I wanted a bag too but as I'd reached my limit I'll have to stick to shoving things in my pockets. You've got good taste, so I'd love to hear from you that I've made a good choice.

Thanks,

Max

Dearest Jean,

You've got to reply straight away, this is serious. What if when Jean comes I get CARRIED AWAY? I suppose it's possible. My self-control's so weak – look what I'm like with Smarties.

It's all Mum's fault for forcing Jean into a hotel. She's so conventional she probably thinks my virginity's safe, so long as I'm back under her roof by night. But I know for a fact that lots of people do it before their official bedtime. Claire Rayner's always telling bored married couples to nip home for a bit in their lunch hour. I could always tell Mum we'd spent the day in a museum and she'd be none the wiser. God I'm scared. What'll I do?

It all started on Pancake Tuesday, when Imelda took me to the evening service at St Joseph's. The priest was talking about what people could give up for Lent. He said that if Jesus was alone in the desert for forty days before being crucified, it wouldn't hurt people to give up sex for that long in sympathy. (Well, I think that's what he meant. He kept going on about 'the special nature of married life', and how you could do without the special bit for a while.)

Then he started in on those of us who shouldn't be in a position to give up sex anyway. The young unmarried ones, he said. Well, he was staring all round the church and finally his eyes settled on me. And stayed there. You know, like I was the one person who really *needed* this sermon. And what's bothering me is that HE'S PROBABLY RIGHT. I didn't realise what filthy thoughts I'd been having about Jean.

The priest said that even if you don't have sex, you can be guilty just for thinking about it. I think about it most of the time. I knew he could tell because I went bright red.

PLEASE write to me *a.s.a.p.* telling me how to keep my Hormones under control. Please, I'm depending on you. Sue's useless. You're the only person I dare ask.

I miss you.

love,

Maxine

PS   I'm glad our bet was never about HOW FAR we go! Thanking you for accepting the new terms. Basing it on marriage makes it *much* purer.

96 Sheraton Road
London N8

April 2nd

Dear Jean,

Thanks very much for your advice on how not to get into trouble. The only trouble is, what if it doesn't work?

I've thought about your advice a lot. I've even thought about the dangers. I've thought about the rotten names. I've thought about the health risks. What I still don't understand is – what if you know all about the horrible things to do with sex and you STILL get turned on?

There must be some reason people do it despite the risks of unwanted babies, abortions, bad reputations, infections, Herpes, Venereal Disease and AIDS. I think it's probably because it can be a lot of FUN. And exciting.

No offence, but your advice wasn't that much different from Mum's. The one good thing you said was, 'If you're not sure, you're not ready'. That got to me. I'd just re-read all my old copies of *Sweet Sixteen* and their agony aunt said that too. She reckons that if it's not the right person, and at the right time in your life, you'll be so tense it won't be any fun. So what's the point?

I think she's probably telling the truth, because from her photo in the mag she looks like a right little raver herself. Dead glam.

I've cheered myself up now so I'll love you and leave you (hah hah).

xxxx

Max

Hornsey
April 5th

12.30 pm

Dear Jean,

It's way past my bedtime but I'm feeling all soft and gooey tonight and wanted to write to you. Today was Mum and Dad's eighteenth wedding anniversary and, despite all their faults, they deserve the best so me and Sue made it a really special day for them.

Seeing as it wasn't a work day we woke them at six thirty to have breakfast in bed. We could have let them sleep later but their bacon and eggs would have got cold. Cooking them didn't take as long as Sue expected. Even though Dad had been on lates, he said, 'Christ, what have I done to deserve this?' He was really touched.

After they got up we settled Dad into an armchair and wrapped a blanket round him so he could read the paper in comfort. Then to make Mum feel a bit younger we did her hair.

Sue was bossy of course so she got to be the stylist and I was just her apprentice. That meant she got to shampoo in the colour and do the blow-dry while I made endless cups of tea and swept the floor. We had a row about that but then I remembered it was Mum's day and nobly shut my gob.

It was worth it, Mum looked lovely. She wasn't too sure about the colour (a sort of punky orangey pink) but we said it took years off her and she cheered up. We wanted to give her a professional make-up too but Mum said we'd spoiled her quite enough for one day, even though Sue's got some gorgeous new oranges and greens. So Sue did my eyes instead and I know I looked great because, later, loads of people in the street stared at me.

Dad was a bit iffy about Mum's hair. He didn't like the colour or all the gel. He said we'd made her look like a candyfloss soaked in chip fat. That must have hurt Mum's feelings so we made him kiss and make up. They were very embarrassed kissing in front of us but dead cute really.

Sue and me had been on at Dad all week to get Mum a really *romantic* present. Guess what he gave her – a jar of face cream!?! Dad said it was specially good for wrinkles. But after Mum hit him, Dad dug into his pocket and got out her *real* present. It was a lovely gold chain with a beautiful little gold heart with '18' engraved on it. It's rolled gold, which is nearly as expensive as proper gold. He hung it round Mum's neck for her, like men do in films, and she looked so chuffed I nearly cried.

I'm so glad my parents love each other. Sometimes I'm not sure but today proved it. They've just been stuck in a rut. You know, staying in every night watching the telly. When I get married I'm going to make sure to keep the romance. We'll have three-course candle-lit dinners every evening and then go down to the pub. When we've got kids I'll get in a nice girl like me to baby-sit and we'll only go out three or four times a week. I think that should be enough.

So that Mum and Dad wouldn't have an excuse not to go out, their present from me and Sue was tickets to the theatre. (You know our family. Dead posh!) You'd have laughed at what we sent them to see – it's called *No Sex Please, We're British*. The lady in the ticket agency said that's what all the anniversary couples go to. I just hope Mum's not too tired to enjoy it. A couple of hours before they went out I found her in the bathroom washing her hair again. She said she was so knackered from her working week it must have slipped her mind that we'd done it already.

Poor old duck. All the gel had come out but at least the colour stayed in. I told her it was guaranteed to last six weeks so that was a consolation. Now I'll turn in – to dream about how I'll be celebrating *my* wedding anniversaries!

Lashings of love

Maxie

PS   I'm glad you ditched Bunsen Burner Pete. Who'd want to be Mrs Peter Ramsbottom anyway?

April 12th

Dear Jean,

I don't *believe* the letter I just got from you. Jean's
arriving in a few days, my nerves are in tatters, my
clothes haven't arrived from the catalogue yet and you
pick NOW to give me another stupid lecture about me
being a stupid snobby Southerner!?! Why??! It's a sick
joke, you saying I'm a snob. You're the one whose
dad's got a pub, you're the one with the big flat, the nice
clothes, a steady job making sandwiches. You've even
got a room of your own and a nan and a dog. It's *me* that
lives in a slum.

I'm dead depressed, worrying about what Jean'll
make of it. I'm sure the real Head of London Transport
doesn't live in a two-bedroom council house with damp
on the walls. I was hoping to steer Jean well clear of
Hornsey, but Mum says he'll think the English dead
unfriendly if we don't do him proud. She's got in
enough Jaffa Cakes to feed him for a week.

Mum and Dad are trying to make it nicer here but it's
a waste of time. Their idea of home improvements is
Dad painting anti-damp stuff on the walls and Mum
decorating them with her favourite letters from Mrs
Thatcher.

Outside is looking better than yesterday but that's not
saying much. Dad's cut the grass and straightened the
gnomes. Sue exerted herself and cleared the hedge of
chip bags. But it's still not the two acres of rose gardens
Jean's expecting.

You should see the new covers Mum bought for her
throw cushions. They're red, purple and yellow
sunflowers on a green background. She says bright
colours are all the rage but what with our couch being

black and white zebra stripes I don't think they go together. Of course I'd never tell Mum that. You should have seen her when she got back from Wood Green, she was just like a little girl she was so excited at buying something new.

AND she bought me a bottle of French perfume. Now I feel guilty. When I think of her slaving all day in that smelly chip shop, then lashing out on me so *I* can smell nice it makes me want to cry. I just did.

Poor Mum. She'd give you the shirt off her back, she never spends anything on herself – and then I've got the cheek to feel ashamed of *her*.

I know it's all my own fault. I should never have lied to Jean. But I did, so what do I do now?

Jean's almost here but that hasn't stopped the rotten teachers setting us end-of-term exams – There are three tomorrow and I haven't done any revision yet. I'll probably fail them all and be expelled. Then I'd really be able to feel sorry for myself.

Please, please, ring – I need you.

Thanks,

Max

Three days before J-Day
(April 16th)

Dearest Jean,

I'm feeling a bit calmer now. Thanks – your phone call helped a lot.

You're right. The best way to play it is to say nothing at all about things being different from I've described. If Jean is as sensitive as I think he is, he won't ask awkward questions. He's so gentlemanly he wouldn't want to show me up. In fact he'll probably feel quite protective towards me. He'll see me as an English Cinderella, and realise that I only exaggerated things because I love him so much and didn't want to lose him. Then he'll feel so guilty about being rich that he'll want to redistribute his wealth by marrying me.

Now that I can see things more clearly, I feel much better. On the other hand, if Jean *does* ask questions, I could tell him that Dad *is* the Head of London Transport but has just turned Socialist. I could say that Dad sold our *château* to raise money for more free bus-passes for poor people. That would show Dad in a good light. And me. I mean, I wouldn't have to sound resentful because we now live in a council house. I'd say it was a real privilege to live so close to the humble, struggling masses that Dad serves. I'd sound such a wonderfully *good* person that Jean would become even more besotted than before.

What I mean is, I couldn't bear to admit to Jean that I lied. It's going to be hard enough sticking up my nose and sucking in my cheeks so that I look more like you.

But it'll be all right. It's bound to be. In the paper today my horoscope said, 'A relative will give you all you need'. I showed that to Sue and told her about the terrible things that happen to people who stand in the way of prophecies. She got scared, and said I could borrow anything I want if my clothes don't arrive from the catalogue in time. That has to be a good omen, Sue being so generous.

Well, I guess this is the last letter from me to you, my very best friend in the whole world, before the course of my life is decided once and for all. Makes you think, dunnit?! If I get the time I'll write to you every day while Jean's here, so you can think of me and beam good thoughts my way.

I'll be thinking of you, too. It's hard not to. Your photo's pasted on to my make-up mirror so I know what I'm supposed to look like.

With much love,

Maxine

A hotel room
Londres WC1

THE MOST WONDERFUL DAY OF MY LIFE
Avril dix-neuvième
(April 19th)

Dearest Jean,

SWOON! First off, Jean's even more good looking than his photo. What a knock-out! He's got enormous soft brown eyes just like a cow's, but sexier. And his hair's dead modern. You know, short at the back and sides but long on the top so that he's always having to flick these black curls out of his eyes. The first time I saw him do that I *nearly* fainted on the spot – DEAD sexy.

But – let's start at the beginning. There was a bit of a mix-up. At the station I was so busy checking Jean's photo that when he did come through the ticket barrier I DIDN'T EVEN SEE HIM. God, you'd have laughed. I was nearly crying, I couldn't see him anywhere. I was hanging over the barrier, looking at an empty platform, when this guy came up from behind and asked in this knee-trembling accent was *I* Maxeeen 'Arrison. There he was!!! In my excitement I forgot to suck in my cheeks and tilt up my nose. But I was dead chuffed – he'd recognised me from your photo!

I couldn't believe that this guy before me, in the pale lemon suit with the big padded shoulders, was only seventeen. He looked like a *real* man. You'd have loved it. It was just like a scene from one of those pink Romance books . . .

'*The look he gave me was scorching. His eyes flickered over me, up and down, up and down, as he inspected me from head to foot. He couldn't take his eyes off me. I could see he was smitten.*

'*I felt so chic in my new clothes. They had arrived only that morning. I hadn't been sure that the green and white trousers and orange lurex top were the right combination, but now I felt more sure than I had felt of anything in my life. Beneath Jean's gaze I felt ravishing.*

'*In his hand lay a photograph. As he looked from it to me and back again his lip curled in a way that was devastatingly manly, devastatingly French. Obviously he couldn't believe his luck that at last we had met in the flesh, and our dream had become reality.*

'*At last I silently nodded "yes" to his question. A look almost of pain crossed his face. Then, manfully, he fought back his desire and gently kissed me twice on each cheek, in the fashion of his country.*

'It was only a fleeting meeting of our flesh — but oh! . . .
' "Yes," I said in a trembling voice, "I am Maxeeen
'Arrison." Then I said, "Let's go for a coffee." Even though I
prefer tea . . .'

WOW!!!

Well, pardner, that's your lot for now. I've written
this in Jean's hotel room while he's recovering by taking
a bath. I've practically dissolved into a puddle myself so
you'll have to wait until later for more news.

My fondest, fondest love,

Maxeen ('Arrison)

96 Sheraton Road
'Ornsey
Londres

le soir, avril dix-neuvième
(the evening, April 19th)

Instalment the second

Dear Jean,

Jean took ages in the bath. He was very put out about
England being so dirty. He spent half an hour telling me
how clean French trains are and how ours aren't even fit
for animals. I agreed. It was a very interesting
discussion. Then I did my bit to clean up Britain's image
by picking bits of chewing gum off his trousers.

No, I DIDN'T see him without them on! Jean only
gave me his suit to clean when he returned in some
other clothes from the bathroom up the corridor. He
was a bit put out that there wasn't a bathroom *en suite*,

but the lady downstairs said what could he expect for £10 a night? At least hot water, I'd have thought. We had to put 50p in a meter for that. Jean hadn't changed his money yet, so I paid. We rang Claridges from the station but Jean said not to bother when I told him the rates. I nearly fainted. My Mum would have to cook chips for three whole weeks to pay for one night there!

Then I had a good idea, and asked one of the station porters where we could find a cheap hotel. He gave me a bit of a funny look then said to try round the back of the station. We did, and then I found out why the funny look. Half of them are used by *prostitutes*! We twigged when they asked at the first hotel if we wanted to rent a room for just one hour or two. Jean thought that was very funny, but I was hurt and DEAD embarrassed. He said it wasn't surprising, given the way I was dressed.

I didn't think I looked *that* dressed up, even if my new shoes did have three-inch spikes. But I felt a bit self-conscious after that so I covered my lovely lurex top with the boring navy blue cardi. I'd never have bought these shoes if I'd been able to tell from the catalogue how high they are. I know that high heels are supposed to make your legs look slimmer, but what's the point if they're both in plaster?

The lady in the *proper* B&B we found was a bit iffy at first too. I'd got my cardi buttoned up to my eyeballs by then, but she still made a point of telling me that she ran 'a very clean house'. She'd got an Irish accent though, so I put her mind to rest by asking where me and Jean could catch Mass tomorrow, seeing as we French are Catholic just like the Irish. She was nicer then but I stole a bar of soap all the same to get my own back. I figured if her house was so clean she wouldn't need it.

While Jean was in the bath I decided I wouldn't let him go any further than Number Two but he didn't even come near me. I was a bit disappointed but slow romances are definitely the best. Anyway, Claire

Rayner says it's no good when you're worried, and Jean was very worried about getting the chewing gum off the seat of his trousers.

By then it was getting on so Jean suggested I ring Mum and say we'd have to give Hornsey a miss. I wanted Jean to enjoy some traditional English food, though, so I took him for a fry-up. After that we walked a bit and Jean played pin-ball in the amusement arcade. I wanted to chat but it was so noisy in there we couldn't talk much. I didn't really mind because I had a dead exciting time watching the way the hairs on Jean's chest quivered as he pulled the levers.

I didn't really mind when Jean didn't kiss me goodnight – Claire Rayner always says tiredness kills romance, and poor Jean *must* have been exhausted after his long journey and four hours on the fruit machines. You have to be understanding about these things.

Poor Jean. It will be easier for us after they've built the Chunnel Tunnel.

I need my beauty sleep more than ever so I'd better go now. But I hope you enjoyed hearing about The Most Wonderful Day In My Life.

With much love from
Your Best Friend

Max

Dearest Jean,

You cheered me up – I *should* write to my MP about
the Tower of London being shut on Sunday mornings.
And the National Gallery, and all the big shops and the
Cutty Sark in Greenwich. As Jean said, we went a long
way today and all for *rien* (nothing). Britain will never
attract enough tourists to become a world power again
if the only thing open on Sunday is Westminster
Cathedral.

I thought the Holy Liturgy of the Mass was very
moving, but Jean couldn't understand it. His English is
non-existent. I think I'll write to the Pope about that.
When the Mass was in Latin Catholics could go
anywhere in the world and still follow it. I expect that
was a great help to girls with foreign boyfriends like
me.

I had a real struggle getting an out of date Easter Egg
off Mr Habib for a present for Jean. He thought it was
for me. He said he didn't want me collapsing over his
Sunday papers and begged me to buy a bar of Diabetic
chocolate instead. He'd got in a whole box just for me,
so I felt obliged to buy three bars and then I ate them.
Tonight I'm two pounds heavier. No wonder my legs
ache, with all the weight on them.

I expect the French don't give eggs to people at
Easter. Maybe I'll get a present later.

Talking of food, you're right, it *was* a good idea to
feed the birds in Trafalgar Square. All the tourists do.
It's not my fault about Jean's flash suit. As you said,
birds will be birds.

Mum's calmed down now. I scrubbed the pots for

her, just to make amends. She shouldn't have kept dinner waiting for us. I told her before I left the house that Jean would probably want to eat somewhere special.

I promised Jean I'd do my make-up different tomorrow, to try and look older.

It was a great day really. Thanks a lot for ringing to share it.

luv u,

Max

Love Land

Monday
(April 21st)

Dearest Jean,

I'm glad to report that today went much better than yesterday. In fact it was one hundred per cent SWOONY!

Well – ninety per cent. Your idea that we go to the horse show in Regent's Park went down like a cup of cold sick. Jean got cold and bored and said the horse dung everywhere smelled awful. I said he was right. The French have a very sensitive sense of smell, that's why they're good at making perfumes. I know you and I loved seeing the big brewery horses last year, but we weren't very sophisticated then. That's probably why we didn't notice the dung. Jean is very sophisticated, that's why he prefers Porsches to horses. What *is* a Porsche? Jean said it like everyone should know what it is, so I didn't like to ask.

Well. Was I ever relieved when I remembered about the fair. Jean was over the moon about the one-arm bandits and played them for hours and hours, and won FOUR QUID! I felt ever so proud of him. And ever so grown-up, draping myself over the machines like I was a gamblers' moll in a casino. It was murder on my blisters.

Jean was pleased with himself too, he got all daring and said we should try to get into a pub. We managed it! Jean had four halves of red wine and I had THREE halves of cider (!?!). I wouldn't have drunk so much but it gave me something to do while he was thinking. Jean's very deep, he thinks a lot. And frowns. He's quite shy really, but I like that in a boy. It proves he's sensitive.

And it gives me time to work out how to translate into French what I want to say. Jean won't speak English, he was quite annoyed when the barman wouldn't take his order in French. Jean shouted back that French is a World Language, that all intelligent people should speak. I thought he sounded a bit like that rotten teacher we had in primary school, who made the Cypriot kids feel stupid for speaking their own language to their mums. But I don't think Jean can *really* be a racist, I mean, he's a foreigner himself.

I was a bit disappointed when we didn't go back to the fair, though. Do you remember the great time you and me had last year, and how we thought it'd be dead romantic to go in the Haunted House with a boyfriend? We thought you could *really* enjoy screaming then. Still, there's always next year. And he's right, the rides are very expensive.

The good thing about going to the pub is that THE BOOZE STOPPED JEAN BEING SO SHY (know what I mean?!). At the bus stop we had a really *great* snogging session. It wasn't like having a slug in your mouth at all – it was so YUMMY I thought I'd melt!

Jean was dead romantic and in a really good mood. He kept calling me his 'leettle Maxeeen', and laughing.

It was wonderful, I felt really feminine and small but safe, squashed up against his huge, strong shoulders. Then the bus came and we waved goodbye, and I ran across the Heath to catch mine. And, no matter what Mum said later, I know that Jean *will* make a fine, and protective, husband. I know that from his shoulders, even if they are padded.

In case you haven't gathered, me and Mum had a row when I got in. She was mad because she'd cooked tea for us again, mad because she could smell the cider, and maddest most of all because Jean had let me cut across the Heath alone so late at night. She said he's no gentleman.

I told her to shut up, that I know how to take care of myself. I do. But there was *one* man I thought was following me, he was coming up closer, and calling out. Even though I felt a bit silly, I took my shoes off and made like the clappers for the nearest doorway. I was all ready to ring the bell or even smash a window to make sure someone came out, but my bus came and I jumped on and saw him disappear back on to the Heath.

I guess I must have been a bit shook up though, or I wouldn't have yelled those horrible things back at Mum, about her being bitter and twisted. But I did, and she swiped me.

Somehow we ended up cuddling, and having a bit of a drunken cry. She'd been at the Spanish Gut Rot again, she said it was better than chewing her nails to the bone while she waited for me. She said the saddest thing that a mother has to do is teach her daughters that the world isn't always safe for them.

She said she was proud I'm brave and adventurous but that I have to be sensible too. I said I wouldn't do it again – I think I meant it – and then I was sick from all the cider and hot dogs and candy floss. Mum was lovely. She wiped my face with a cold wet flannel and put me to bed, just like I was little again. It was really nice.

Now I've sobered up a bit, which is why I can write to you. And I can't sleep. I have to bring Jean home to tea, Mum says, so I guess I'll have to. D–Day is the day after tomorrow, when Dad comes off lates. I feel sick again, just thinking about it. Otherwise, I feel wonderful. Kissing your own special 'man' is everything I ever dreamt it would be!

I wish you were here so we could talk properly. I miss you,

Max

Tuesday April 22nd
9 pm

Dearest best-friend J,

I'm knackered. Jean must have gone into every shop in Oxford Street today. Still he was happy and that's what counts. Thank God the shops were finally open, that's all I can say. He bought STACKS of clothes! Three jumpers, two pairs of trousers, five shirts AND a gift-pack of briefs (I didn't know where to put myself when he was buying those!).

Jean wanted me to have some new clothes too, in fact he insisted. He found some beautiful classy clothes that he said would look much better than mine. But I couldn't afford them, so all I bought was some blusher.

I got a bit confused, trying to help him work out the difference between English and Continental sizes. Jean wasn't very pleased either that I kept tripping over him. But with these heels I couldn't catch my balance especially as I had to keep my left hand in my pocket all the time. So that the assistants wouldn't notice that I hadn't got my wedding ring on. I was pretending I was his wife, you see. One assistant was very sweet, she said she could tell from the tone of Jean's voice that we'd been married a long time.

God, my feet ache. Jean was very protective about them. He found some lovely shoes for me, that were comfortable *and* pretty. I got MY FIRST PRESENT FROM JEAN! I didn't have enough for the shoes so he bought me a box of plasters. Then he told me to go into the loo and to put them on, and sponge my tights. He said the blood from my blisters looked disgusting. He's so sensitive, he was really upset for me.

Got to go now and soak my feet before they fall off. I'll have to try Sue's tip and stretch them with potato slices.*

lotsa luv,

Max

PS *My shoes, I mean, not my feet!

THE CAPITAL OF ENGLAND
Wednesday April 23rd

Dearest J,

Do you like this new stamp of Princess Di? Jean says if I didn't eat so much I could be as thin as her. He says the French really admire her, as she's the only Brit with good taste. I think Fergie's very stylish too so I felt hurt on her behalf. Also the Queen's.

Jean didn't like the Changing of the Guard today, he'd been expecting tanks charging up and down the Mall. He said I should know by now that he'd had enough of horses. I pointed out that these were different, they were Royal, but Anglo–French relations became severely strained by six horses in a row unloading just opposite us.

He was also cross that the Queen didn't come out to wave. The flag was flying and he said that if she was at home today she should be up on the balcony earning her keep. I said, 'At least the British have a sense of History', but thought 'That is more than can be said for those nationalities who spend all their time in shops'. (Today = 1 pr jeans, 2 prs shoes, 5 prs socks, 5 pckts mints.)

Then it was Now or Never – we were due for tea in Hornsey. On the bus I tried to prepare Jean for what he would find. I rabbited on, in a roundabout way, about how my recent conversion to Catholicism had guided me to realise that helping the poor mattered more than possessions. I was dead nervous. But Jean fell asleep while I was talking. He told me later that it was the sound of my voice that did it. I think I must have been talking too quietly. And, as I had hoped, Jean was much too sensitive to enquire about our family's change in circumstances.

Mum's grub was great. She'd gone all patriotic so tea was ever so English. We had cottage pie, chips and peas, Orangeade and then ice cream with Chocolate Flakes stuck in. Sue had got in paper serviettes, and kept slipping saucers under the cups when Mum forgot them, and we acted like we were this sophisticated all the time.

Dad had on his wedding suit and did his best, apart from asking Jean had the French got electric light yet. I pretended to translate that but didn't.

It was a bit difficult having to be the translator for

everyone. I did what I could with Mum's and Sue's questions, but as Jean didn't have a lot to say for himself there wasn't much to translate back. So I made a lot up, all about how much he liked our house and food and them and me and London and our Queen. Sue asked how come it took me so long to say in English what Jean took so little time to say in French. I told her that the words in French are all very short.

After a while though I found it hard to keep inventing Jean's conversation, so I didn't really mind when Jean left after only an hour and a half. It had been a strain on everyone. Especially on me. The worst was when Mum gave Jean a souvenir London bus and Dad went into a mad mime. I know Dad didn't know that he's supposed to be the Head of London Transport, but he could have been more subtle. He made me, Mum, Sue and Jean all sit in chairs lined up one behind the other, while he dashed up and down pretending to ring the bell and dishing out tickets like he does when he's working.

I don't *think* Jean twigged. And when we said goodnight by the hedge he was very sweet, saying he would always be grateful to me and my family. I asked him why, and he said that now he knew it really was true about the English being eccentric. I suppose Jean would think it eccentric to give all your money away to the poor. God forgive me for running him down, but if he has one fault it's that he's a bit tightfisted.

Jean didn't kiss me goodnight, but maybe he was put off by knowing that Mum, Dad and Sue were looking through the nets. I could tell because they'd switched off the light inside so they could see into the dark better.

It was a very nice day. Apart from the no kissing, I mean.

luv an' hugs,

Maxine

HQ of the Bring-A-Tourist-To-Hornsey
Campaign
Slogan, 'See Hornsey and die'

Thursday April 24th

Dear Jean,

You're never going to believe this, but today my
rotten Mum made me make Jean spend the day in rotten
old boring Hornsey. She says that Jean's bound to be
interested in where I come from (I can't think why, I'm
not). The real reason is she's worried it costs too much,
me gallivanting up town.

Little does she know. Don't tell anyone, but do you
remember that Post Office savings account Mum
opened for me? Well, it's nearly empty now.

So – here is a potted version of our 'action-packed',
cheapo tour of Hornsey.

10.30 am
Jean was worried about getting lost, so I fetched him
from his B&B. I had an interesting discussion with the
landlady about French Catholicism while he spent an
hour deciding what to wear.

11.45
Number 14 bus from Kings Cross to Hornsey. V.
good, Dad wasn't on it.

12.30
Lunch. V. bad, J. chose Mum's chip shop. Bert the
owner said Mum in the back, washing up. Offered to
fetch her. I winked madly at Bert. Bert twigged and
sized J. up. Said 'Mum's The Word, Ha Ha'. I pretended
that was funny. Worth it, Bert gave us free fish and
chips. I told J. that was because I once rescued Bert's
little girl from drowning.

12.35
Bert's little girl came in. Dawn is twenty-five.
Scarpered before she could say hullo.

12.45–1.45
Ate food, wandered about, I pointed out local
landmarks. J. pointed out ten lots of dog turds. Told J.
very good the French so clean, but why *bidets* in the
bathroom just for washing their feet? J. fell about,
explained *bidets* really for washing their BITS. The rude
ones, I mean. Decided I'd kill Sue when I saw her.

1.45–2.30
Town Hall exhibition on One Hundred Years Of
Hornsey. Boring but free.

3.00–4.00
Sue's boutique. All the girls fancied J., wanted to
measure his inside leg. Felt jealous, but didn't know
what an inside leg is, or how to measure it. Cheered up
when Sue said J. not allowed to leave the shop without
buying her little sis a present. Sue not a bad sister really.
She even gave J. discount. He bought 1 pr jeans, 3
T-shirts. Sue said discount on the hairband he bought
for me so small not worth deducting.

4.15–5.00
Park. Put on hairband and danced on the bandstand, like
when I was little. Sue says boys like it when you're
childish. True. J. very sweet, stopped being cool and
played in a sandpit.
    Discovered it was a dog toilet. V. upset.

5.30–7.30
Emergency baby-sitting for Amanda and Nathan. Glad.
Now J. would see how much I love kids. Little Sods
horrible, wouldn't let me get ready for disco in peace.
Allie gave me a lecture on make-up being sexist. Seb

ruined my blusher using it as war paint. Allie gave him lecture on Cowboys and Indians being racist. Both told me to use their proper names.

Earned enough for approx. half a cider.

8.00–11.30
Under Eighteens Disco. Lots of girls from school there, me very proud of being with J. Him yummy in tight new jeans and tight new shirt, lots of chest hair showing.

Only problem, J. cross because no booze. Frankie saved the day, smuggled in cider in lemonade bottle. J. not v. grateful. I'd thought they'd get on because both Catholics. No go. Frankie's sure motorbikes are faster than Porsches. J. said the Irish are mad. Frankie said the French are snobs.

Broke up fight by suggesting dance. J. too tired. Danced with Frankie. Not bad. In fact quite dishy. He wild over my lurex top. J. didn't act jealous but Imelda sure he was. She said French are passionate but hide it.

Irish passionate and don't hide it. Frankie sang Irish rebel songs at J.'s bus stop and cop car stopped. I said J. the French Ambassador's son, and big diplomatic hoo-ha if missed the last bus. Cops scared, drove away. Bus came, J. went.

No time for kissing.

12.30 am (now)
V. confused. Also v. v. sad. Hoped J. would propose tonight at Disco. But not even one smoochy dance.

Heart leapt then, when letter-box clattered, and one red rose fell on to mat. Thought sent by J. by late-night Interflora. But note saying 'For an English Rose', smudged in motor oil, so must be from Frankie. Probably remembered me sad on St George's Day because the English never wear their national flower. Sweet.

Tomorrow J.'s last full day, and last chance to get him to propose. Rate I'm going, not much chance. Know I didn't want him to go too far, but just one snog is ridiculous.

Yours, despondent, unloved and confused,

Maxie

On the Circle Line
Friday, April 25th
6 pm

Dearest Jean,

I've been sitting on the Underground for the past hour, just going round and round. I'm dead worried. Jean is expected home for a farewell tea but wouldn't come.

He said he didn't want to spend his last night in London in Hornsey. I left him outside the amusement arcade in Leicester Square. Jean wanted me to stay, but I said we shouldn't both let Mum and Dad down. Anyway, I'm sick of him playing those machines when I haven't got the money to play them too.

As it was his last day, Jean chose a really posh restaurant in Covent Garden. I only had an omelette and cup of tea. It set me back £6 and I didn't even get chips. Only salad. I didn't enjoy the sodding omelette either, being so worried about the bill. God knows what I'll do for money now. The first instalment on my catalogue clothes is due tonight!

Jean had told me he had to be careful because he was saving up for a Porsche so I didn't mind about him never paying for me before. *Now* I know what a

Porsche is. It's not a bicycle, it's a really flash car! He isn't hard-up, he's just mean! I must need my head examining. He said he needed good clothes for his career but today he forked out £80 (EIGHTY!) for a hand-made jumper from a trendy stall. Even I know that when he's a lawyer he won't be able to stand in court wearing a jumper saying 'I luv Princess Diana'.

Covent Garden's posey, I hate it. I started to tell Jean about how it was years ago, when it was a real market, a fruit and veg one. Before I realised what I was doing, I was telling him about Grandad being a porter there and how, before he scarpered on the family, he used to carry Mum around in a basket on his head when she was little.

I've always loved that story. But as soon as I said it I knew I'd blown it about us being posh. I panicked, and thought about spinning him some yarn but then I thought – bugger it, why should I? I've worked out what's wrong with Jean – he's a snob.

Why should I lie just to get on the right side of a snob? Probably a snob doesn't have one. Whatever you say or do or have they'll always find a new way of putting you down. Mum's right, she's always said that people should take you as you are.

Today I caught Jean sneering at something and suddenly I thought, 'Well, mate, you're dead good looking and all that, but I'm Maxine Harrison and you can like it or lump it. And if you don't like it, that's *your* loss.'

Then we walked past the London Transport museum in Covent Garden, and I thought that would be as good a place as any to tell him the truth about Dad's job. You see, I've also had it up to here with Jean being rude all week to other bus conductors. I'd been thinking about that time Dad helped a woman have her baby on his bus, and about the other time when he and his driver were dead brave and drove a busload of screaming yobbos straight to the cop shop. I'll bet no pen-pushing businessman like Jean's father ever risks his life on the job.

Well – I *did* mean to tell Jean all this, but I've got to admit I chickened out. I know Honesty's the Best Policy and all that, but when you've told as many lies as me it's hard to know how to start putting it right.

Well, not lies really, just fibs.

I suppose if I'm going to be more Mature in the future I'd better start by getting myself home. I just hope Mum and Dad aren't too hurt. Or mad. Especially with me.

Yours, sadder but wiser,

Maxine

96 Sheraton Rd
Hornsey
London N8

Friday, 11.30 pm
late

Second instalment

Dearest Jean,

I feel so full of love I HAVE to tell someone. It's Mum and Dad you see. They've really cut me up. No, they didn't give me a rocket when I got in, they were so dead nice it hurt. And Mum had gone to such a lot of trouble too – you should have seen the cake, she'd iced a British flag and a French flag on it, all sort of intertwined. She's usually too busy to bake, but Dad told me she'd done it at night after I'd gone to bed so that it would be a surprise.

Well, that really finished me off. I'd been spinning Mum and Dad a yarn about Jean getting sick from our foreign water, but when I saw that cake I just burst into tears and told them the truth. Well, sort of.

Dad started mouthing off about inconsiderate foreigners but Mum gave him an eyeful and he went all sensitive instead. I think they must have had one of their 'Little Talks' about me. Anyway, he took me into the back garden to take my mind off things and got me to help him with some weeding. 'Pass the trowel,' he'd say, and then mutter something about there being lots more fish in the sea or how I was almost as pretty as a flower.

He didn't really cheer me up, he's my dad so he's bound to think me pretty, but he meant well and that's what did me in. I felt such a traitor, not sticking up for him.

Ditto Mum. She'd even got another present for Jean, a tea tray with a picture of Andrew and Fergie on it. For his Mum and Dad. I gave them a box of *Ma Cherie* chocolates saying it was for them from Jean, from Paris. Actually I bought them from Mr Habib. He let me have them on tick.

Then Linda came round for her catalogue money but I managed to fob her off at the door. I didn't really lie, I just said Mum was out and I couldn't talk right now because I was suffering from Emotional Exhaustion. That's what the papers always say is wrong with pop stars when they're having nervous breakdowns.

Even Sue was nice, and lent me her second best shoes, so my blisters don't get any worse.

Got to go now. Sorry this is another depressing letter. Anything I write ought to carry a Government Warning, 'Letter Reading is dangerous for your Mental Health'.

Got to go now,

Bye

M.

JUST AFTER SEEING JEAN OFF
(April 26th, 11 am)

My dearest one and only Jean,

Please wash your hands after you have read this. I am writing it in a toilet. I just couldn't wait to tell you the good news. Jean's gone and I DON'T GIVE A DAMN! Really!

Now my blisters can heal. I brought my flatties in a plastic bag to the station, and the minute I'd waved him off, I dashed in here to change. I nearly didn't wear the heels to the station, but I couldn't resist giving Jean one last peek at my legs. I want him to feel sick as a pig about what he'll be missing.

I don't want him to suffer too much, but I wouldn't mind if he is as sick as a pig for a while. Give him his due, he did look a bit ashamed when I gave him a slice of the cake Mum had baked for him. I presented it on the Fergie and Andy tea tray, with a little servile curtsy. Then I said that if he didn't like Mum's gifts he was welcome to throw them under the wheels of the train. I said that we wouldn't mind because it was 'well known that the working class don't have feelings'.

I said all this with a big smile, like it was a joke, but I wanted him to know that I'd twigged how snotty he is and that I'd never let him get away with it again. I know that there'll never be another opportunity but I don't care. I only cried for five minutes in the Super Bogs before I started to feel relieved, and five minutes is nothing.

I'm glad I was proud. Jean tried to give me a last kiss, but I pulled away. I said I was going down with Hay

Fever, and didn't want to give him germs. Pulling away from those big manly shoulders was one of the hardest things I've ever had to do. He still looked gorgeous in his suit, even if it was more mustard than lemon coloured after a week in London. We both said we'd write, and we both knew we never will.

Even if he is a snob he'll always have a place in my heart. I don't think I'll ever be able to throw away Jean's photo.

My First Love – gone. Forever. Oh damn, now I've made myself cry again.

Don't worry about me, I'm not really heartbroken. But please write or ring AS SOON AS YOU GET THIS.

I miss you, my one and only Jean,

Maxie

The Liar's Retreat
London N8

Sunday April 27th
Dinner time

Dearest Jean,

PLEASE ring me. I'm even more miserable today than yesterday. It's Linda's fault. She bumped into Mum at Mr Habib's this morning and asked if I was over my nervous breakdown. Obviously she too knows the true meaning of Emotional Exhaustion. Mr Habib overheard and sent me round a Get Well card and a bar of Diabetic chocolate. Mum guessed why I'd fobbed Linda off. She made me show her my Post Office savings account book. Then she beat me up with the *Sunday Express*.

I was crying so loud that Dad came in. I tried telling him that I'd donated the money to the Labour Party, but he called me a Bloody Little Liar and threw the *News of the World* at me. Now they've stomped out to the pub and I've got to have dinner ready for them when they come back. I've been crying so much the potatoes are soggy and I haven't even cooked them yet. If Jean hadn't been so mean and snobby I wouldn't be in this mess. I'm so confused, I don't know who to hate most – Mum, Dad, Jean or me.

I'm back up to nine stone nine as well. Probably tomorrow I'll be even fatter. I ate half the skin off the chicken when I was basting it. The oven timer has just pinged and there's still no sign of Mum and Dad. Probably they'll blame me if the dinner is burnt. Child–beaters are like that, totally unfair.

Please ring me. I know I've said it before, but this time I really need you.

love (platonic – the only kind I now believe in)

Max the Mashed

London

April 28th

Dearest Jean,

If you hadn't rung I don't know how I'd have got through the last thirty-six and a half hours. Apart from the Maloneys and Amanda and Nathan, you are the only person in the whole world who is talking to me. I don't know how I got through school, pretending everything was normal and that I'd recovered. At least I had a reason for looking pale and sickly.

Afterwards I felt so lonely I even went round and offered to sit on the Little Sods for free. Unfortunately Amanda couldn't see that this was really A Plea for Help, and she took me at my word. I spent two hours at the park trying to prevent them from killing each other. Alexandra tried to hang Sebastian by twisting the chains from the swings around his neck. Sebastian tried out the see-saw with Alexandra under instead of on top of it. I bribed them into better behaviour by buying them Flying Saucers and licorice pipes and other things that aren't Good For Them.

Then I felt very sorry for myself and my lost childhood. I remembered you who shared it with me and felt inspired again. Then I remembered that you are going to be a rock star and I wrote a song specially for you. It is all about our friendship. You can set it to music, and use it as your signature tune.

OPENING TRACK FOR THE DÉBUT ALBUM OF
JEAN OGLETHORPE

The North's answer to Miss Piggy (only kidding!)

Lyrics
Maxine Harrison

Music
Still waiting to be written

Title
MY BEST FRIEND

Boys may come
and boys may go
but only you
me really know

we tell each other
everything we do
and sharing secrets
we never rue

when others mock
or treat us cruel
a best friend's smile
is like winter fuel

We used to have
our ups and downs
our arjy barjies
our little frowns

but now we're older
we see the light
and try our best
not to fight

for being friends
makes us strong
and when times are tough
helps us along

so all in all
I've just this to say
to the nicest friend
who's ever come my way

dogs may come
and dogs may go
but a *girl's* best friend
is you I know

Isn't that great?! i.e. just like you. I can't wait to see
you sing it on *Top of the Pops*.

I luv u

Max

114

Dearest J,

Now I feel even guiltier. Mr Habib told me that Mum
has asked for her Christmas Club money back. That
means she has to use it to pay Linda for the catalogue
clothes. Also we won't be getting any Christmas
presents. So Mum and Dad aren't lying when they say
we're poor and that I'm an irresponsible lying thief. I
feel terrible. I have bankrupted my own family.

I went round to Imelda's and begged her to take me to
Confession, so I could tell the priest my sins. But she
said only real Catholics can go and that she'd go to Hell
if she took me. She is totally lacking in Christian
charity.

Imelda's brother Frankie is much nicer. He heard me
crying and burst in and said *he* didn't mind going to Hell
if that made me happier. Well, he didn't quite say that,
but he did say he'd finally got his scooter to work and he
wouldn't mind spinning me down the hill to St
Joseph's.

Confession was great and so was the scooter. I felt
just like a girl in a film with my hair streaming out
behind me. Frankie gave me some quick tips before I
went in, on what to say to the priest, so I didn't get it *all*
wrong. Frankie says he sometimes makes his sins up if
he can't exactly remember them all, but I've done so
many it took me ten minutes just to get through the
main ones.

I can't tell you *what* I confessed, seeing as you're not a
Catholic. But let's just say that after a while the Priest
interrupted me to ask if I was *married*. (Me, married? At
fourteen?!) When I said I wasn't, he said it would help

115

Take My Mind Off Things if I did some Good Works. As for the compulsive lying, he said it was a stage young people go through and he was sure I'd grow out of it as I got older. He asked how old I was and I said seventeen. I'm sure God *has* forgiven me because the statue of the Virgin Mary smiled at me.

Got to go now – I've a Social Studies essay to do for school and I want it to be really good. I've decided now that I won't be a pilot, I'll be a Social Worker instead. They do lots of Good Works and don't have to be good at Physics.

love, from your Best Friend in Christ

Maxine Harrison

A Working Class Area of London

Bank Holiday Monday 5th
The official version of May 1st, The Workers' Day

Dear Comrade Jean,

Wait till I tell you all my good news!
1) I have got a job.
2) Mum and Dad are speaking to me again.
3) I have become a Dangerous Extremist.
4) I have got a new Admirer.
5) I have given up vice.
To expand:

1) ON MY HAVING A JOB
After Confession I told Frankie all my woes and he said he would think about them. Next morning he came round and told me to put on my best clothes. I put on my orange lurex top, which I was already wearing.

Then he took me round to the supermarket where he humps boxes at weekends. AND NOW I HAVE GOT A JOB THERE TOO! I am going to be its cleaner. It's strictly illegal seeing as I'm under age but the manager is desperate. The health inspectors have given him a month to clean up or close down. There is rat poison everywhere. Working alongside Frankie will be lovely.

2) ON BEING LOVED AGAIN BY MY FAMILY
I have promised Mum and Dad I will pay back Linda and the catalogue from my cleaning job. They're very pleased. Mum celebrated with Spanish Gut Rot and Dad patted me on the head and sang 'The Red Flag'. So we're back to being a normal, happy family again.

Even Sue was nice. To protect me against industrial hazards she gave me a bottle of nail strengthener. It was only half used, so that was generous. She said she didn't want me to lose my claws or she'd have no one to fight with. I was quite touched. That is the nearest Sue has ever come to admitting she loves me.

3) ON BECOMING A DANGEROUS EXTREMIST
I have been on my first DEMONSTRATION! We all went, Mum, Dad, me, Sue, Frankie, Imelda and all the little Maloneys, Amanda, Nathan and the two Little Sods from round the corner. And we didn't even have to pay on the bus. Dad showed his London Transport pass and said, 'It's for May Day, mate', and the conductor let us all off. There were sixteen of us. Then we went to a demonstration to complain about the run-down of London Transport. It was great, none of the pigeons in Trafalgar Square shat on anybody.

Mum got quite carried away, she was shoving leaflets at all the passers-by, even though they had a cartoon showing Her Friend Mrs Thatcher hacking away with an axe at a bus full of Old Age Pensioners. I told her I'd write to Maggie Thatcher and tell on her and Mum

looked quite worried, then said, 'Well, I've got to help
protect your Dad's job. I'm sure she'd do the same for
Dennis'.

Then, in the crowd, Frankie and me lost Mum and
Dad and all the others and had to get home on our own.
Frankie paid for me. He said it was a gesture of
solidarity seeing as until Friday night, when my new job
starts, I'm still one of the unemployed.

He's very kind.

And sensitive, and clever. I told him about wanting to
be a Social Worker. It sounded boring as soon as I said
it. Frankie agreed. He said he wants to be an entertainer,
so why don't we form a double act? Then we could do
good and have fun at the same time, by singing ditties
on the dole queues. We made up loads on the bus.
Here's one:

Even though your Giro's late
and your larder's empty
Even though it makes you sick
that the middle class have plenty
Even though your clothes are torn
and the SS says that's baloney
there is no need to feel forlorn
when you can hum with Frankie Maloney

Isn't that great?! You can tell Frankie really cares about
people. He says that's because he's the eldest of a large
family. Although he only wants four kids himself. I
agreed. In today's economic climate, having a big
family is not sensible. Also four is my lucky number.

4) ON MY HAVING A NEW ADMIRER
You'll never guess who's asked me out!!??!!
FRANKIE!!! He's taking me to a Gaelic football match
on Saturday.

How will I get everything done before then?! I've got

to clean my clothes, my shoes, my hair, my room, and there's only five days till Saturday. Do you think I can wear my orange lurex top to a Gaelic football match? Ring me AS SOON AS YOU GET THIS LETTER AND TELL ME!!!

5)   ON GIVING UP VICE

I'm making a start with gambling. Whatever happens between me and Frankie, I'm not going to call in our bet. It's caused you and me enough grief already. How about cancelling it, Pardner?

Now that I am more Mature than in my Jean days (can it really be only two weeks since I saw the last of him? Yuck), I don't think that having a boyfriend is the only thing that matters.

lotsa luv,

Maxine

PS   Whaddya think of Maxine *Maloney* as a name??!!

A NOTE FROM THE AUTHOR TO THOSE NOSEY READERS WHO ALWAYS WANT TO KNOW IF A STORY IS TRUE:

The characters in this story are entirely fictitious, or sort of. They bear no resemblance to anyone living or dead, except when I couldn't be bothered to make things up.

Special thanks are due to my editor, Carole Spedding. She asked me to write this book so if you want someone to blame you can pick on her. Her patience in the face of missed deadlines has, like her friendship over many years meant a great deal.

Thanks also to her teenage daughter, Natasha 'Keep it in the family' Spedding, who as our Youth Consultant read the manuscript many times. We would like to place it on record that this was of her own free will. Any allegation that she is an Exploited Child Labourer is entirely unfounded.

One last thanks to Alison Burns, editor with a different publishing house, for putting me on the right track.

grab a livewire!

real life, real issues, real books, real bite

Rebellion, rows, love and sex ... pushy boyfriends, fussy parents, infuriating brothers and pests of sisters ... body image, trust, fear and hope ... homelessness, bereavement, friends and foes ... raves and parties, teachers and bullies ... identity, culture clash, tension and fun ... abuse, alcoholism, cults and survival ... fat thighs, hairy legs, hassle and angst ... music, black issues, media and politics ... animal rights, environment, veggies and travel ... taking risks, standing up, shouting loud and breaking out ...

... grab a Livewire!

For a free copy of our latest catalogue,
send a stamped addressed envelope to:

The Sales Department
Livewire Books
The Women's Press Ltd
34 Great Sutton Street
London EC1V 0DX
Tel: 0171 251 3007
Fax: 0171 608 1938

Also of interest:

Eileen Fairweather
French Leave
Maxine Harrison Moves Out!

'Dear Jean,
I don't want you worrying unnecessarily, so I am writing
to reassure you about my future. I haven't got one. My
disgusting parents broke the news to me the minute I
walked in the door . . .'

Maxine Harrison knows all about hardship. Her best friend lives
203 miles away, she's suffering major exam stress – and her
boyfriend's more interested in his motorbike than her. Now her
parents claim they're too poor to keep her in school. It looks like
her future's selling knickers at M&S.

There's only one solution: to Leave Home . . .

'Outrageously funny . . . Maxine's resilience gives us all a
lesson in how to cope.' *7 Days*

'Very good indeed.' *Vogue*

Fiction £3.50
ISBN 0 7043 4916 7